COMPACT *Research*

Hallucinogens

by Crystal McCage

Drugs

ReferencePoint
Press™

San Diego, CA

Foreword

A s modern civilization continues to evolve, its ability to create, store, distribute, and access information expands exponentially. The explosion of information from all media continues to increase at a phenomenal rate. By 2020 some experts predict the worldwide information base will double every 73 days. While access to diverse sources of information and perspectives is paramount to any democratic society, information alone cannot help people gain knowledge and understanding. Information must be organized and presented clearly and succinctly in order to be understood. The challenge in the digital age becomes not the creation of information, but how best to sort, organize, enhance, and present information.

ReferencePoint Press developed the Compact Research series with this challenge of the information age in mind. More than any other subject area today, researching current events can yield vast, diverse, and unqualified information that can be intimidating and overwhelming for even the most advanced and motivated researcher. The Compact Research series offers a compact, relevant, intelligent, and conveniently organized collection of information covering a variety of current and controversial topics ranging from illegal immigration to marijuana.

The series focuses on three types of information: objective single-author narratives, opinion-based primary source quotations, and facts and statistics. The clearly written objective narratives provide context and reliable background information. Primary source quotes are carefully selected and cited, exposing the reader to differing points of view. And facts and statistics sections aid the reader in evaluating perspectives. Presenting these key types of information creates a richer, more balanced learning experience.

For better understanding and convenience, the series enhances information by organizing it into narrower topics and adding design features that make it easy for a reader to identify desired content. For example, in *Compact Research: Illegal Immigration*, a chapter covering the economic impact of illegal immigration has an objective narrative explaining the various ways the economy is impacted, a balanced section of numerous primary source quotes on the topic, followed by facts and full-color illustrations to encourage evaluation of contrasting perspectives.

The ancient Roman philosopher Lucius Annaeus Seneca wrote, "It is quality rather than quantity that matters." More than just a collection of content, the Compact Research series is simply committed to creating, finding, organizing, and presenting the most relevant and appropriate amount of information on a current topic in a user-friendly style that invites, intrigues, and fosters understanding.

Hallucinogens at a Glance

Hallucinogen Use

Teens and young adults are the most frequent users of illegal hallucinogens in the United States.

Decline in Hallucinogen Use

While the rise in the number of teens who had tried hallucinogens in the late 1990s is significant, national data indicates that this number is currently in decline.

Hallucinogen History

Hallucinogens were used by ancient cultures in religious and spiritual ceremonies and have been used for similar purposes all over the world for thousands of years. Hallucinogens were synthesized in the twentieth century and researched for their possible therapeutic benefits.

Therapeutic Hallucinogens

Scientists continue to explore the possibility of using some hallucinogenic drugs such as LSD as treatments for alcoholism, post-traumatic stress disorder, and depression. LSD can also be used to help terminally ill patients find comfort at the end of their lives.

Ceremonial Hallucinogens

It is currently legal for members of the Native American Church to ingest peyote as a part of their religious ceremonies, even though it is illegal for anyone outside of this organization to do so.

International Bans on Hallucinogens

Most hallucinogens are illegal in Australia, Canada, and most European countries. As with the United States, in spite of calls for more research on such drugs these countries do not see any medical uses for them.

Hallucinogen Abuse

In 2004, hallucinogens were the third most commonly abused illicit drug in the United States, behind marijuana and cocaine. Approximately 1 million Americans reported using hallucinogens.

Health Effects

With the exception of ecstasy, most scientists agree that hallucinogens are not that dangerous physically. The biggest danger of hallucinogen use is altered perception, which can lead to accidental death and suicide.

Legalization

A growing number of scientists are calling for a revision of federal policies that list hallucinogens as Schedule I substances. They argue that more research is needed on these drugs. Others argue for legalization of all drugs, including hallucinogens. Legalization would allow these substances to be regulated, thus reducing crime and making the drugs safer. However, recent surveys indicate that a majority of Americans are against drug legalization.

Overview

66 Scientists have learned a lot about LSD, DMT, mescaline, psilocybin, MDA and MDMA (ecstasy) since the psychedelic '60s, when people blatantly consumed vast quantities of mind-blowing drugs. But research advances are usually reported in the *American Journal of Psychiatry, Synapse or Molecular Pharmacology*, and not many regular hallucinogen users (past, present, future) subscribe. So lots of people still believe the federal, for-the-moronic-public's-own-good anti-drug campaign misrepresentations that originated in the '60s—that LSD breaks chromosomes, causes flashbacks and drives people insane or to suicide. None of that's true. It never was. 99

—Cheryl Pellerin, *Trips: How Hallucinogens Work in Your Brain.*

66 Abuse of these psychedelic drugs is a serious concern—one of the potential side effects is death; however, based on the rarity of this occurrence, individuals can be lulled into believing these substances are not life threatening. 99

—Sophia F. Dziegielewski, *Understanding Substance Addictions: Assessment and Intervention.*

For thousands of years a variety of cultures all over the world have used hallucinogens in religious and spiritual ceremonies. These cultures used hallucinogens to gain spiritual insight. For example, the

LSD, shown here in paper, or blotter, form, is a synthetic hallucinogen and is probably the most well known. Each square, or "tab," is equal to one "hit."

Vedas, which are arguably the oldest surviving texts in the world, mention a holy drink called Soma. Many believe this drink is made from a hallucinogenic mushroom. And for hundreds of years, aboriginal groups have used hallucinogenic plants to, according to David M. Grilly "promote group cohesiveness, spirituality, and mystical experiences."[1] These hallucinogens were naturally occurring and came from a variety of mushrooms and other plants.

Synthetic hallucinogens were developed in the twentieth century. In the late 1920s scientists began researching psychoactive plants for their possible medical benefits. In 1938 chemist Albert Hofmann invented a synthetic hallucinogenic drug, LSD. For five years, the psychedelic properties of LSD were unknown. But in 1943, Hoffmann accidentally gave himself a dose of LSD and discovered its effects. Following World War II, scientists, doctors, and psychiatrists explored the medical and therapeutic benefits of hallucinogenic drugs, but when researcher Timothy Leary introduced drugs like LSD to the public, accidents occurred and governmental authorities became concerned.

In the last few decades a large number of teens used hallucinogens at parties called "raves." It seems clear that people are fascinated with hallucinogens. However, many controversies surround these drugs, and their use can sometimes be dangerous.

The Term *Hallucinogen*

Most scientists agree that the name *hallucinogens* is not necessarily the best name for the drugs in this class. Many hallucinogens do not necessarily cause hallucinations but instead alter users' thoughts and moods, perhaps making them more relaxed or more connected to a god or other people. Additionally, high doses of many substances can bring about hallucinations in people. Some scientists and researchers now call the drugs in this class *psychedelics*, but *hallucinogens* is still the most common term. The general consensus among scientists seems to be that hallucinogens bring about some kind of altered state and may sometimes bring on hallucinations at low doses that are below the toxic level.

Hallucinogens affect the neurotransmitters in the brain. There are four basic categories of hallucinogens, which are based on the type of neurotransmitter they affect.

Four Basic Categories of Hallucinogens

The first category of hallucinogens, serotonin-like hallucinogens, consists of the drugs that affect the serotonergic receptors in the brain. Serotonin plays an important role in mood, sleep, appetite, and sexuality. Some hallucinogens in this category occur naturally. Ergot, for example, a fungus that grows on many plants, is very similar to LSD. Psilocybin is another naturally occurring serotonin-like hallucinogen found in mushrooms. LSD is the most well known of the serotonin-like hallucinogens and is synthetic, or created in a lab.

Norepinephrine-like hallucinogens are the second category of hallucinogens. Norepinephrine is a chemical that the body releases under stress, such as in a dangerous situation or even worrying about an upcoming test in school. Norepinephrine-like hallucinogens occur naturally and have been created synthetically. Mescaline is the active ingredient in a small cactus called peyote, which grows in the deserts of Mexico and the southwestern United States. MDMA, or Ecstasy, was synthesized in 1912 but did not become popular until the 1970s after people exploring its therapeutic benefits in psychotherapy spread word about it to the public. Ecstasy may be the most well known of the norepinephrine-like hallucinogens today because of its increased popularity in the 1990s.

Many plants all over the world are acetylcholine-like hallucinogens. At low doses these hallucinogens create mind-altering states but are quite deadly in high doses. This class of hallucinogens can cause an overdose of norepinephrine and adrenaline (in the blood stream) leading to panic, high blood pressure, and possible stroke. The two most common acetylcholine-like hallucinogens are atropine and scopolamine, which are derived from highly toxic plants called nightshades, and mandrake, a member of the same nightshade plant family. While synthetic forms of these substances exist, these drugs are used in a far different way. They are used for ailments like diarrhea. The natural derivatives are combined with pharmaceuticals such as sulfate to make the drugs more

Mescaline is the active ingredient in this small, spineless cactus called peyote, which grows in the deserts of Mexico and the southwestern United States.

stable, but the natural substances have proven much more effective than the synthetic.

Glutamate-like hallucinogens affect glutamate in the brain. Involved in learning and memory, glutamate is the most abundant excitatory neurotransmitter (neurotransmitters that stimulate and excite) in the human central nervous system. Although glutamate occurs naturally in many foods, its effects are not as dramatic as those produced by the synthetic form. The drugs phencyclidine (more commonly known as PCP) and ketamine are glutamate-like hallucinogens. Originally developed as anesthetics, they caused patients to have no memory of their surgery, But memory loss is not usually desirable and is a negative side effect of the recreational use of PCP and ketamine.

History

Scientists first researched the potential benefits of hallucinogenic drugs to treat headaches, depression, and alcohol addiction. For example, scientists studied LSD as a possible aid in the cure for mental illness. Synthesized hallucinogens transitioned from medical research to public consumption during the 1960s. In 1961 Timothy Leary and Richard Alpert received a research grant from Harvard University to study the therapeutic benefits of LSD. LSD was still legal, so using it in scientific research was considered legitimate. Leary and Alpert began to share LSD with others and supported public use of the drug.

> " Scientists first researched the potential benefits of hallucinogenic drugs to treat headaches, depression, and alcohol addiction. "

During the 1960s and 1970s young people began using hallucinogens recreationally, and accidental deaths occurred. People accidentally overdosed or hurt themselves while high on the drugs. Researchers who had hoped for possible medical benefits from research on hallucinogenic drugs had their hopes dashed when the U.S. government made the drugs illegal, even for research in most cases.

In 1968 federal Drug Abuse Control Amendments were changed to make LSD, mescaline, psilocybin, and other hallucinogens illegal. Most hallucinogens are listed as Schedule I substances. Federal law defines Schedule I drugs as highly addictive, dangerous, and without legitimate medical uses. While hallucinogenic drugs can be dangerous, some scientists and researchers, such as Albert Hofmann and Alexander Shulgin, believe this designation is too harsh. Hallucinogens are not addictive and the drugs had never been fully examined for their potential medical uses, these critics argue.

Benefits Recently Discovered

New studies of hallucinogens in the last 20 years have shown some benefits of the drugs. For example, LSD has been studied as a treatment for alcoholism, and MDMA, or Ecstasy, has been studied as a treatment for post-traumatic stress disorder. According to an article in the *Newsletter of the Multidisciplinary Association for Psychedelic Studies*, an organization promoting further research on hallucinogens, "The push to re-evaluate the government's policy has come from researchers who contend that under carefully controlled conditions, hallucinogens have been shown to benefit the terminally ill, alcoholics, and some psychiatric patients."[2]

Dangers of Hallucinogens

Hallucinogens can be very dangerous. Some of the hallucinations that the drugs induce have caused people to hurt themselves. Flashbacks are another dangerous side effect of hallucinogenic drug use. Flashbacks occur when users experience trips even when they are not on the drug. Flashbacks have been known to traumatize people, and for some people they never seem to go away. Another danger is the bad trip. A bad trip occurs when a user experiences traumatic, panicked feelings and sees grotesque images while under the effects of a hallucinogen. One anonymous user describes how traumatic it can be when a trip goes badly. He posted the experience on a Web site sponsored by Erowid called the Vaults of Erowid. Erowid is a member-supported organization with the goal of providing accurate and nonjudgmental information about psychoactive drugs.

> **Flashbacks have been known to traumatize people, and for some people they never seem to go away.**

I started to get anxious, and everything seemed wrong. I've had it before, it's a common reaction, you just ride it out. But this felt a lot worse and was coming on fast. I spent the next couple of hours worrying like crazy, convinced I'd hurt myself badly. After a few hours I calmed down, but I still felt all wrong. I was in control, but my head was just telling me something was going wrong, and it was intense. . . . The next day was the worst feeling, when you wake up and your head is just on fire. I had a massive headache, it was ringing like nothing else and I still felt really anxious and was shaking. By now I was really scared. . . . I don't know if it was nervous exhaustion, but my vision started to slow down and get blurry. I couldn't eat or sleep anymore. I was completely exhausted but couldn't sleep. I was in that state you get when you're coming down off E [Ecstasy] and you just want to drift off but you can't. I went and saw a doctor and he told me not to worry, it'd wear off, but I didn't believe him. I thought I had brain damage. I was off work for a week and I'm on anti-depressants now. Two weeks later I feel much better, though still slightly on edge and down.[3]

These bad trips can be frightening and can affect users for years after the bad experience. Although some users point out that bad trips are rare, they are a reality for many hallucinogen users.

> The peyote ritual is protected by law as are a few other rituals involving hallucinogen use by other organized religious groups.

Ceremonial Uses of Hallucinogens

The Native American Church is perhaps the most recognizable organization to use hallucinogens for ceremonial purposes. Although the beliefs of individual tribes can vary greatly among the Native American Church, many tribes practice a ritual involving peyote, especially when there is need for contemplation. The ritual consists of prayer, song, and eating peyote.

Members of the Native American Church believe that the ingestion of peyote helps them come closer to God. The peyote ritual is protected by law as are a few other rituals involving hallucinogen use by other organized religious groups. While statistics on the Native American Church are uncertain, it is estimated that more than 50 tribes in the United States continue to practice the peyote ritual.

Extent of Use in the United States

In the 1990s hallucinogenic drug use in the United States increased dramatically as drugs like LSD and Ecstasy became associated with all-night dance parties called "raves." According to the U.S. Department of Justice, "Between 1991 and 1996, the percentage of Americans who had used psychedelics at least once in their lives grew from 6 to 14 percent." Moreover, research from the U.S. Department of Justice linked this rise in hallucinogen use with the growth of raves, "underground dance parties that cater to those under age 21."[4]

It is speculated that raves existed in the United States for years before their rise in popularity in the 1990s. What is certain is that during the 1990s raves became a part of mainstream youth culture. Although raves do not always incorporate the use of illegal drugs, the use of hallucinogens such as LSD and Ecstasy has been and continues to be common at these parties. Ravers, usually young people in their teens and early twenties believe that hallucinogenic drugs heighten the experiences of the lights, music, and feelings of togetherness that are associated with rave parties. Overdoses are a problem at raves, as are reports of exhaustion and dehydration as ravers who are high on the drugs continue to dance while their bodies struggle to deal with the effects of the drugs.

> " Ravers, usually young people in their teens and early twenties, believe that hallucinogenic drugs heighten the experiences of the lights, music, and feelings of togetherness that are associated with rave parties. "

National surveys indicate that the rise and decline of hallucinogenic drug use has coincided with the rise and decline in popularity of raves.

The University of Michigan's Institute for Social Research Monitoring the Future Survey indicates that the number of twelfth graders who reported using LSD peaked at 13.6 percent in 1992. It also reported that the number of 12th graders who reported using hallucinogens other than LSD peaked at 10.7 percent in 2001.[5] Since that time, hallucinogenic use by teenagers has declined, and raves are not experiencing the popularity they once had.

Decline in Use of Hallucinogens

National surveys indicate that this is due to efforts to curtail hallucinogen use. According to surveys by Monitoring the Future, the percentage of high school seniors who reported using LSD at some time during their lives fell from 13.6 percent in 1997 to 10.9 percent in 2001 and was down to 3.3 percent by 2006. Reported use of Ecstasy also fell, though not to the levels that LSD did. Reported use of Ecstasy fell to 6.5 percent in 2006.[6]

Law Enforcement and Hallucinogens

As the use of hallucinogenic drugs has declined, law enforcement has been less of an issue for local, state, and federal agencies. However, law enforcement officers, particularly at the local level, have continued to control drug use and focus attention on teenage drug use at raves. Research has helped in this area, and local communities for whom raves are an issue will often have undercover officers who monitor teen rave culture and communication systems, as well as behavior at the raves themselves.

Prevention and Treatment

Most hallucinogens are not physically addictive, as no withdrawal symptoms occur after use is discontinued. However, research suggests that they can be psychologically addictive. Treatment efforts include therapy and long-term counseling. Most drug treatment centers that provide treatment for physically addictive drugs like heroin and crack will also provide treatment for hallucinogenic drug use. But prevention remains a focus for any kind of drug use.

Many drug prevention programs are available in the United States. The federal government sponsors drug education programs to educate teachers, parents, and local law enforcement officers. When hallucinogenic drug use reached alarming levels in the late 1990s, the federal government launched major media campaigns designed to appeal to teens and twenty-somethings, who were the biggest users of the drugs. Recent surveys indicate that prevention programs appear to be working, as numbers have declined in recent years.

Legalization Issues

There is debate about whether hallucinogenic drugs should remain listed as Schedule I substances by the federal government. Some advocates, including Shulgin, go so far as to say that hallucinogens should be legalized. Those in favor of legalization contend that many of the dangers and crimes associated with halluci-

> " **Most hallucinogens are not physically addictive, as no withdrawal symptoms occur after use is discontinued. However, research suggests that they can be psychologically addictive.** "

nogenic drug use and trafficking would be eliminated or greatly reduced if the drugs were legalized and regulated. A big concern among users is the quality and purity of the drugs. Hallucinogenic drugs are most dangerous when mixed, and since the drugs can only be purchased illegally, quality cannot be assured. Essentially, every time a user takes one of these drugs, he or she is taking a chance that the drug will be impure. Any crime associated with trafficking would also be eliminated, as the government could regulate distribution.

Even those who do not support the full legalization of these drugs call for a reclassification of them. One such organization is the Multidisciplinary Association for Psychedelic Studies, which promotes scientific research on hallucinogenic drugs. It cites historical and recent research indicating potential benefits from hallucinogens and wants more freedom to conduct research. At this time, because of the Schedule I classification, it is quite difficult to get permission to do research on these drugs, and only a few permits for research are released each year.

Still, governmental organizations such as the U.S. Drug Enforcement Administration contend hallucinogenic drugs are dangerous and should not be legalized or reclassified. Although reported deaths from overdoses are few, suicides and deaths from accidents during trips have occurred. There is also no way to predict a bad, or traumatic, trip. While research indicates that good and bad trips are related to setting or place, there are many other variables. Sometimes the mood of the user affects the trip. Some research indicates that some people are simply more prone to bad trips because of their personality type, and a first-time user would have no way of knowing if his or her personality would be more prone to a bad trip. Bad trips have been shown to lead to depression and affect people for years due to flashbacks. Because of these dangers, it is difficult for some people to imagine ever legalizing these drugs.

> **As the legalization debate continues, so do efforts to secure further research on the possible medical and therapeutic benefits of hallucinogens.**

As the legalization debate continues, so do efforts to secure further research on the possible medical and therapeutic benefits of hallucinogens. While the dangers of hallucinogen use in uncontrolled settings remain clear, a growing number of researchers from all over the world are interested in and calling for more research. Although hallucinogens remain illegal and tightly controlled by the federal government, they have been a part of human culture for a long time, and they will continue to be in the future.

What Are Hallucinogens?

66 Hallucinogens comprise a unique collection of substances that are ingested to induce alterations of consciousness . . . when ingested in nontoxic doses. Hallucinations are usually visual, auditory, and tactile, in varying combinations, depending on the substance ingested, the setting, and the experiences of the person using them. 99

—Joseph A. Salomone III, "Toxicity, Hallucinogens."

66 The two chemicals which are of most use in creating a change of consciousness conducive to spiritual experience are mescaline and lysergic acid diethylamide (known, for short, as LSD). 99

—Alan Watts, "The New Alchemy."

Hallucinogens have been a part of human cultures for thousands of years. Dried peyote has been found in Texas that dates back to approximately 5000 B.C., and archaeologists have identified cave paintings and sculptures from three different continents that depict different kinds of hallucinogenic mushrooms and plants. According to Richard Evans Schultes, executive director of the Botanical Museum of Harvard University, "The use of hallucinogenic substances goes far back into human pre-history. There have been suggestions that even the idea of the deity might have arisen as a result of their weird and unearthly effects on the human body and mind."[7]

> **The word *halluci-nogen* is derived from the Latin term *hallucinari*, which means 'to wander in the mind,' but not all drugs classified as hallucinogens cause hallucinations.**

Hallucinogens are a class of drugs that have been historically difficult to name and classify. The word *hallucino-gen* is derived from the Latin term *hal-lucinari*, which means "to wander in the mind," but not all drugs classified as hallucinogens cause hallucinations. Many may alter moods and thoughts. Moreover, high doses of many other substances can cause hallucinations; therefore, it is quite difficult for sci-entists to decide what actually consti-tutes a hallucinogen. However, most scientists agree the essential criterion is that the drug elicits an altered state at a nontoxic, low dose.

What Are the Different Types of Hallucinogens?

Although scientists sometimes disagree about the best way to organize the different kinds of hallucinogens, one way they are classified is by the effect they have on the mind and body. This type of classification is based on the neurotransmitter (a chemical substance released from a neuron) that they affect or resemble. The first category is the group that affects serotonin in the brain. Serotonin plays an important role in mood, sleep, appetite, and sexuality. The second category is the group of hallucinogens that are similar to norepinephrine. Norepinephrine increases heart rate, blood pressure, breathing, blood sugar levels, and adrenaline. The third category influences acetylcholine, involved in many systems such as memory, digestion, breathing, and energy storage. The last neurotransmitter discussed is glutamate, which is the most im-portant excitatory chemical in the brain. It is what keeps us awake and makes learning possible.

What Are Serotonin-Like Hallucinogens?

Serotonergic receptors in the brain are influenced by substances such as lysergic acid diethylamide (LSD), psilocybin, dimethyltryptamine (DMT), and bufotenin. LSD is a synthetic hallucinogen and is probably the most well known. Psilocybin is found naturally in several species of mushrooms in North America. Dimethyltryptamine is metabolized in small amounts in the body and occurs naturally in some species of plants, such as reed canary grass and harding grass, which are found in the southwestern United States. Bufotenin was originally isolated from the toxic secretions of certain toads, such as *Bufo alvarius* (commonly referred to as the Colorado River toad) found in the southwestern United States and northern Mexico. The venom of this toad is smoked as part of a sacramental rite practiced by a religious organization called the Church of the Toad of Light, but some people simply lick the toad.

Lysergic Acid Diethylamide (LSD)

In the 1940s Swiss scientist Albert Hofmann discovered LSD while searching for new medicines. Hofmann was trying to duplicate the effects of ergot, a naturally occurring form of LSD, when he accidentally exposed himself to one of his experiments, known as "LSD-25," and experienced strange sensations. He then tried a larger dose and experienced what Dr. William McKim refers to as "the first LSD trip."[8] Although Hofmann's records of his first experiences with LSD indicate that he was clearly distressed by his experiences, he continued to experiment on himself with the drug, finding a more appropriate dose. He has remained one of the biggest and most well known supporters for scientific research on LSD and other hallucinogenic drugs.

> " In the 1940s Swiss scientist Albert Hofmann discovered LSD while searching for new medicines. "

For many years scientists researched the benefits of LSD and other hallucinogens in patients who were struggling with mental illnesses. Scientists hypothesized that LSD could help these patients recover repressed memories and learn to accept themselves. In the 1960s psychologists Timothy Leary and Richard Alpert, both of Harvard University, began to experiment with the therapeutic effects of LSD but then began to share LSD with the public. They used themselves as subjects, as well as local artists, students, and other academics. University officials and parents of students were upset over Leary and Alpert's research, and Leary and

Alpert were dismissed from Harvard. Both went on to become famous advocates for hallucinogenic drug research and personal use. Together they founded the International Foundation for Internal Freedom. Leary would later found a religion called the League for Spiritual Discovery that used LSD as a holy sacrament. Despite arrests and imprisonment, Leary continued throughout his life to argue that drugs like LSD provided people with important spiritual and therapeutic benefits.

Psilocybin Mushrooms

Psilocybin mushrooms are sometimes referred to as "magic mushrooms" and were thousands of years ago considered sacred by some cultures, particularly those native to the regions of the southwestern United States and Central America. Psilocybin use increased as a recreational drug in the 1960s but never became as popular as LSD. These mushrooms continue to be used as recreational drugs. Like LSD, psilocybin has been studied for its medicinal purposes. Leary and Alpert studied psilocybin as an aid in psychotherapy. In 2001 the Food and Drug Administration (FDA) approved a U.S. study researching psilocybin as a treatment for obsessive-compulsive disorder, or OCD. Some researchers hypothesize that OCD is related to impaired serotonin regulation and that psilocybin's effects on the serotonergic receptors may prove beneficial in treating OCD symptoms.

> " Psilocybin mushrooms are sometimes referred to as "magic mushrooms" and were thousands of years ago considered sacred by some cultures, particularly those native to the regions of the southwestern United States and Central America. "

Dimethyltryptamine (DMT)

Dimethyltryptamine occurs naturally in many plants, especially those found in South America. Shamans of Amazon tribes used it for spiritual and medicinal purposes. These native smoked or snorted the plants. It was first synthesized in 1931, but its effects were unknown until 1956 when it was understood to be a hallucinogen. When smoked or injected into the bloodstream, DMT produces the mystical and spiritual experiences often associated with Native American cultures. However, DMT will not have these effects when eaten unless accompanied by another drug, an MAOI (monoamine oxidase inhibitor). MAOIs make more DMT available to affect the brain because they stop the production of enzymes in the body that breakdown DMT; however, they also increase other neurotransmitters like serotonin, which can have dangerous side effects, including mania, increased heart rate and blood pressure, and stroke.

Bufotenin

Other serotonergic hallucinogens, like bufotenin, also have long histories of use. Ancient cultures supposedly used the secretions of Bufo toads for shamanistic purposes, and during the Middle Ages Bufo toads were thought to be powerful cure-alls for many diseases and sicknesses. On a more sinister note, these toads were also believed to be important for spell casting, and so were suspected ingredients in witches' brews. Bufo toads, also referred to as Colorado River toads, can be found today in the southwestern United States and northern Mexico, though their population is dwindling due to pesticide use and habitat loss. People smoke the Bufo toad's venom to achieve desired hallucinations, but the toads are also sometimes licked. Problems occur when people mistakenly lick the wrong species of toad. The common cane toad is sometimes mistaken for the Colorado River toad. Because the cane toad's venom contains powerful heart steroids, heart attacks and death can result from licking them.

What Are Norepinephrine-Like Hallucinogens?

Norepinephrine is released naturally when the body encounters a stressful event. Along with the hormone epinephrine (adrenaline), norepinephrine affects the "fight or flight" response, where heart rate and breathing are increased, as is muscle readiness. Naturally occurring norepinephrine-like hallucinogens include mescaline and myristin, found in nutmeg. Synsethsized norepinephrine-like hallucinogens include methylenedioxymethamphetamine or MDMA, commonly reffered to as Ecstasy, and dimethoxyamphetamine or DOM, which is commonly referred to as STP (serenity, tranquility, and peace). Mescaline has a long history of use in religious ceremonies, and synthetic drugs like MDMA and Dimethoxyamphetamine (DOM) have been researched for their medical and therapeutic benefits.

Mescaline

Mescaline is the active ingredient in a small, spineless cactus called peyote. This plant grows naturally in the deserts of Mexico and the southwestern United States. Mescaline may initially produce nausea, vomiting, and tremors, but these symptoms are followed by visions and other sensory hallucinations.

> **Mescaline is the active ingredient in a small, spineless cactus called peyote.**

Mescaline has been used for centuries as a mind-changing drug in religious ceremonies. In South America the Aztecs used peyote, and Native Americans in Mexico and the United States have used peyote for hundreds, perhaps thousands, of years. When Christianity was introduced, some southwestern Native Americans combined it with their religions, incorporating peyote into a new religion, formally called the Native American Church. The U.S. Congress made peyote a legal part of the Native American Church ceremonies in 1970.

Methylenedioxymethamphetamine (MDMA), or Ecstasy

MDMA, or Ecstasy, is a synthetic mescaline-like drug. MDMA stimulates release of serotonin, dopamine and norepinephrine in the brain. This results in euphoria, high energy and strong sensations. It can also result in brain damage, dehydration, kidney failure, and dangerous overheating. This can actually cause muscle cells to burst. It also increases blood pressure by constricting blood vessels. This can rupture capillaries in the brain, leaving pinpoint holes throughout the cortex from the death of serotonergic cells. These dangerous effects most likely happen when users are already overheated and dehydrated from heavy activity like dancing. This is why these drugs are particularly dangerous at raves.

MDMA was patented in 1914 by the Merck drug company, but was not considered very useful because scientists did not know about its effects. It was first used only as an aid in the synthesis of another chemical that helped control bleeding. MDMA was used therapeutically in the 1970s after chemist Alexander Shulgin introduced the drug to a psychotherapist named Leo Zeff. Shulgin is credited with popularizing MDMA by his scientific research on its benefits in treating depression and post-traumatic stress disorder. It appeared on the drug scene in the 1960s but was not illegal in the United States until 1985. It became a popular recreational drug in the early 1980s at expensive "yuppy" bars in the Dallas, Texas, area and at gay dance clubs.

Even after MDMA became illegal in 1985, some research studies continued to explore its therapeutic uses. However, psychotherapists abandoned its use in the 1990s with the discovery that it kills nerve cells. Nevertheless, because Ecstasy creates a sense of euphoria and energy, its illegal use has been increasing among college and high school students in the United States and parts of Europe.

Dimethoxyamphetamine

Dimethoxyamphetamine is also known as STP, which allegedly stands for "serenity, tranquility, and peace." While DOM is less effective than LSD, it is 100 times more potent than mescaline. According to Shulgin, the effects can last 14 to 16 hours. DOM was developed as a class of amphetamines believed in the 1930s to be helpful in treating asthma and hyperactivity. It was never used pharmaceutically but was briefly popular recreationally.

STP has not had the popularity of LSD, partly due to its long-lasting, intense "high." This caused users to panic when the drug was first introduced in the Haight-Ashbury District of San Francisco in the late 1960s, resulting in a frenzy of emergency-room visits. The other downside of STP was the convulsions that could result in death, a side effect not found with LSD.

> 66
>
> **The other downside of STP was the convulsions that could result in death, a side effect not found with LSD.**
>
> 99

Myristin

Myristin, derived from nutmeg, is also a norepineprhine-like hallucinogen, although most people know it as a culinary spice.

While small amounts of nutmeg are safe and produce no physical or neurological side effects, large doses, due to the myristin, can bring about hallucinations similar to mescaline. The use of nutmeg as a hallucinogoenic drug is rare because the amount required to reach an altered state induces vomiting, muscles tremors, deep feelings of dread, and short-lived psychosis.

What Are Acetylcholine-like Hallucinogens?

A number of plants fit into this category of hallucinogens, including deadly nightshade and jimsonweed. Many contain alkaloids that are anticholinergics, meaning they block the effects of acetylcholine, a neurotransmitter responsible for muscle movement, breathing, digestion, and memory. The three most common alkaloids are atropine, scopolamine, and mandrake, all derived from deadly nightshade plants. Atropine is extracted from *Atropa belladonna.* Scopolamine is found in jimsonweed or Jamestown weed. Mandrake is extracted from *Mandragora.* At low doses these cause mind-altering states but are potentially deadly in large amounts. In large amounts the chemicals cause panic, hyperventilation, irregular heartbeat, increased blood pressure, and stroke.

Throughout history, these naturally occurring drugs have been associated with magic and were considered aphrodisiacs because of their indirect effect on sexual arousal. Some historians think that the hallucinogenic effect of these drugs are behind the myth.

Atropine was used to dilate eyes, which was thought to make women more beautiful (*bella donna* means "beautiful woman").

Mandrake had been used for centuries as a painkiller and anesthetic. The root of the mandrake resembles a human form, and this added to its supernatural significance. It was believed that if the mandrake root was removed too quickly or roughly that the mandrake would shriek terribly and cause harm to humans. Historical references to mandrake abound from the ancient Greeks through the Middle Ages, and even modern references refer to mandrake's supernatural qualities, including J.K. Rowling's Harry Potter series.

What Are Glutamate-Like Hallucinogens?

The main hallucinogenic drugs that affect gluatamate are phencyclidine, known as PCP or angel dust, and ketamine. Effects vary by dose, starting with excitement, confusion, and disorientation leading to hallucinations and eventually coma.

PCP and ketamine were used as anesthetics originally. PCP was developed in 1956 as an anesthesia for humans but was discarded because of undesirable side effects, many of which looked like schizophrenia, such as agitation and delirium. Ketamine has similar effects. While these drugs do stop nerve cells from delivering pain messages, their main benefit is the amnesia they cause by blocking glutamate's role in forming memories.

How Are Hallucinogens Used Today?

According to the U.S. Department of Justice, hallucinogen use in America rose significantly in the 1960s and 1970s. In 1974, 17 percent of Americans reported using a hallucinogenic drug in their lifetime. Among teens and young adults, use during one's lifetime rose to 20 percent in 1977 and 25 percent in 1979, then declined during the 1980s. Use climbed again in the 1990s, but recent surveys indicate that hallucinogenic drug use is once again in decline.

In the last decade, more research has been conducted on the benefits of hallucinogenic drugs, despite the concerns that have been raised about potential dangers. However, because hallucinogenic drugs are not addictive, *Science News* recently reported that scientists are looking into using them for "psychotherapy, addiction treatment, and creativity-promoting programs." In one study examining the spiritual benefits of psilocybin, researchers administered doses of psilocybin to 36 healthy adults. Twenty-five of the participants in the study experienced positive, "spiritually significant events," and two months after the study, 29 participants "reported moderately or greatly increased well being."[9]

The drugs described in this chapter have been and continue to be used to treat a wide variety of psychological disorders and general ailments.

> " PCP was developed in 1956 as an anesthesia for humans but was discarded because of undesirable side effects, many of which looked like schizophrenia. "

Primary Source Quotes*

What Are Hallucinogens?

> **If we could sniff or swallow something that would, for five or six hours each day, abolish our solitude as individuals, atone us with our fellows in a glowing exaltation of affection and make life in all its aspects seem not only worth living, but divinely beautiful and significant, and if this heavenly, world-transfiguring drug were of such a kind that we could wake up next morning with a clear head and an undamaged constitution—then, it seems to me, all our problems ... would be wholly solved and earth would become paradise.**

—Aldous Huxley, *The Doors of Perception*, 1953.

Huxley was an English writer born in 1894. He was a prolific author of novels, short stories, essays, poetry, and travel writing.

> **There is good historical evidence that shamans of northern European tribes used mushrooms to induce hallucinations as part of rituals and healing.**

—Hazel Muir, "Party Animals," *New Scientist*, 2003.

Muir has written prolifically about a variety of science topics. *New Scientist* magazine brings science and technology news to the public.

* Editor's Note: While the definition of a primary source can be narrowly or broadly defined, for the purposes of Compact Research, a primary source consists of: 1) results of original research presented by an organization or researcher; 2) eyewitness accounts of events, personal experience, or work experience; 3) first-person editorials offering pundits' opinions; 4) government officials presenting political plans and/or policies; 5) representatives of organizations presenting testimony or policy.

"Acid [LSD] is not for every brain—only the healthy, happy, wholesome, handsome, hopeful, humorous, high-velocity should seek these experiences. This elitism is totally self-determined. Unless you are self-confident, self-directed, self-selected, please abstain."

—Timothy Leary, from *I Have America Surrounded: A Biography of Timothy Leary,* by John Higgs, 2006.

Leary, a researcher from Harvard University who became well known after he shared the hallucinogenic drugs from his research with the public, is one of the most famous supporters of hallucinogens. He responded with the above quote when President Richard M. Nixon called him the "most dangerous man in America" in the late 1960s.

....

"The use of peyote for religious or recreational purposes is not without risk."

—Kurt B. Nolte and Ross E. Zumwalt, "Fatal Peyote Ingestion Associated with Mallory-Weiss Lacerations," *Western Journal of Medicine,* June 1999.

Nolte and Zumwalt work for the Office of Medical Investigator at the University of New Mexico School of Medicine. The preceding quote was taken from an article about a man dying after drinking peyote tea.

....

"The human mind is a mysterious and complex thing. There have never been dependable ways to get into it, take it apart, and see how it works. My hope is that psychedelic compounds may be the tools . . . that can throw some light on elusive questions about how the mind works."

—Alexander T. Shulgin, "Abused Substances," *Technology Review,* August 2005.

Shulgin, sometimes referred to as the "stepfather of Ecstasy," is a pharmacologist and chemist who has studied many hallucinogenic drugs for their benefits in disorders such as post-traumatic stress disorder.

....

66 The dizziness and sensation of fainting became so strong at times that I could no longer hold myself erect, and had to lie down on a sofa. My surroundings had now transformed themselves in more terrifying ways. **99**

—Albert Hofmann, *LSD: My Problem Child,* 1980.

Hofmann, a Swiss scientist known as the "father" of LSD, accidentally discovered the psychedelic LSD while working with ergot alkaloids in 1943.

66 LSD is now taken in smaller doses [than in the 1960s]. The effect is a euphoric high similar to that of marijuana, and powerful mind-altering states are neither desired nor achieved. **99**

—William A. McKim, *Drugs and Behavior: An Introduction to Behavioral Pharmacology*, 2003.

McKim is a professor of psychology at Memorial University of Newfoundland.

66 We have been deeply touched by our experiences with psychedelics and it is hard that there is not a single legal study with LSD given to humans anywhere in the world. **99**

—Rick Doblin, "LSD: The Geeks Wonder Drug?" *Wired*, April 2006.

Doblin is the founder of the Multidisciplinary Association for Psychedelic Studies, an organization supporting the legalization of many hallucinogenic drugs.

66 **There is growing evidence that chronic, heavy, recreational use of ecstasy is associated with sleep disorders, depressed mood, persistent elevation of anxiety, [and] impulsiveness and hostility.** 99

—Michael John Morgan. "Ecstasy (MDMA): A Review of Its Possible Persistent Psychological Effects," *Psychopharmacology*, October 2000.

Morgan is currently professor of visual psychophysics at City University in London. He is the author of an award-winning book titled *The Space Between Our Ears: How the Brain Represents Visual Space.*

66 **Little is known about the long-term effects of hallucinogenic use. Part of the problem is that many users . . . take a variety of other drugs, so it's hard to tease out the specific effects of psychedelic drugs.** 99

—Randy Dotinga, "Peyote Won't Rot Your Brain," *Wired News*, November 4, 2005.

Dotinga is a freelance writer who covers medicine and science topics for *Wired News* and other publications such as the *Christian Science Monitor.*

66 **Under very defined conditions, with careful preparation, you can safely and fairly reliably occasion what's called a primary mystical experience that may lead to positive changes in a person.** 99

—Roland Griffiths, "Hallucinogen in Mushrooms Creates Universal 'Mystical' Experience," *NewsTarget*, September 2006.

Griffiths is a professor of neuroscience, psychiatry, and behavioral biology at Johns Hopkins University.

66 **Perhaps to some extent we have lost sight of the fact that LSD can be very, very helpful in our society if used properly.** 99

—Robert Kennedy, 1966. Quoted in *Acid Dreams: The CIA, LSD, and the Sixties Rebellion*, Martin A. Lee, 1985.

Kennedy was a younger brother of President John F. Kennedy. He served as U.S. attorney general from 1961 to 1964 under President Kennedy.

What Are Hallucinogens?

- The common flower the **morning glory** makes ololiuqui. This chemical is one-tenth as potent as LSD but also causes severe vomiting, headaches, high blood pressure, and drowsiness, so is not popular for recreational use.

- Bufotenin, the hallucinogen derived from **toads**, can also be made in the human body. This is a metabolic error that occurs when the breakdown of serotonin malfunctions. Some disorders linked to metabolic bufotenin in the brain are autism and psychosis, as well as violent criminal behavior.

- Poisoning with ergot, the natural source of an LSD-like hallucinogen, causes symptoms of intense burning in the hands and feet because it constricts blood vessels. From medieval days, this was called "**St. Anthony's Fire**," after a hermit who was said to have similar symptoms caused by the devil's torments.

- **PCP** (phencyclidine, or angel dust) affects glutamate, the most common excitatory neurotransmitter in the brain.

- Carlos Castaneda wrote several books about his hallucinogenic experiences with a Yaqui shaman named **Don Juan**. These books made peyote very popular during the 1960s and 1970s; however, it has been found that the stories were all fiction.

Trends in Hallucinogenic Use by Students

The Monitoring the Future study from the University of Michigan tracked the historical use of hallucinogens other than LSD among high school students. The study found that use peaked in the late 1970s and declined dramatically during the 1980s. The survey indicates the number of students who reported using a hallucinogen other than LSD in the past 12 months leveled off at the turn of the twenty-first century. Numbers are still significantly higher than they were at the lowest levels of the early 1990s.

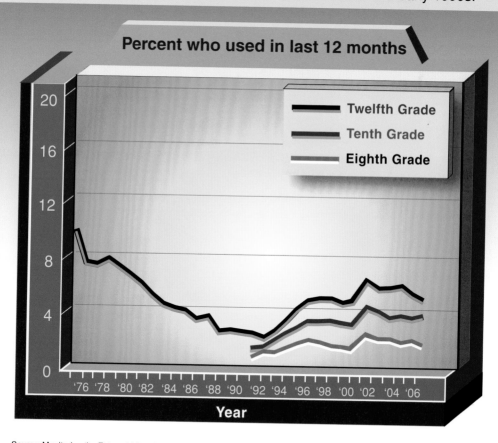

Percent who used in last 12 months

Source: Monitoring the Future, University of Michigan, 2006.

LSD Use by Students Peaks in 1990s

A survey from the Monitoring the Future study indicates the number of students who reported using LSD in 2006. The study found that use peaked significantly in the 1990s. The percent of students who reported using LSD was higher in the 1990s than in the 1970s, when the drug was originally popularized. The survey also indicates that the number of students using LSD since the year 2000 has sharply decreased.

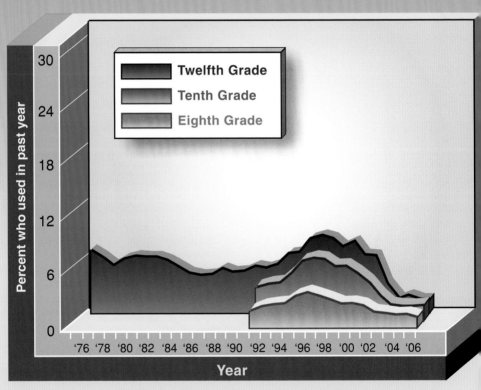

Source: Monitoring the Future, University of Michigan, 2006.

- The 1970s rock band Chicago had a cryptic reference to hallucinogens in the song "**25 or 6 to 4**." Many people thought the title made no sense, but it has since been clarified as "25 or 26 minutes to 4 a.m. and I can't sleep" due to the insomnia caused by mescaline.

- Ecstasy, the common name for MDMA, comes from the **Greek** word *ekstasis*, which translates to "the flight of the soul from the body."

- Like nutmeg, another common spice called mace has hallucinogenic potential. The active chemical is elemicin. Similar to mescaline, it has the nasty side effects associated with too much nutmeg: severe nausea, vomiting, and acute **psychosis**.

LSD Less Available to Students

Surveys of students in the eighth, tenth, and twelfth grades indicate that LSD has become much less available. In the mid-nineties over 50 percent of twelfth graders said it was easy to get. However, in 2006 less than 30 percent felt the same.

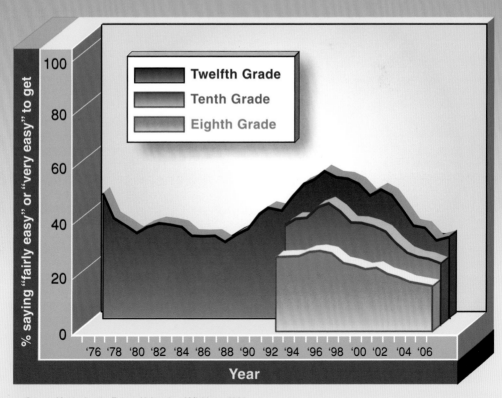

Source: Monitoring the Future, University of Michigan, 2006.

Natural Growing Areas for Peyote

This map shows regions of Mexico and Texas where the spineless peyote cactus grows. Peyote grows along the Rio Grande River that separates Texas and Mexico and farther south into Mexico toward San Luis Potosi.

Source: Edward F. Anderson, "Botany of Peyote," *Peyote, the Divine Cactus.* Tucson: University of Arizona Press, 1980.

- Amanita mushrooms contain potent anticholinergic hallucinogens. They have been used for **thousands of years** by nomadic herders in Siberia. The chemical can be passed through up to six people and still affect the user "spiritually."

- Rabies acts in the same way as anticholinergic hallucinogens such as belladonna do but with fatal results if the disease is left to run its course. Some argue that the effects of rabies may have contributed to **werewolf** legends, as rabid wolves were the source of many wolf attacks in Europe, with the victims becoming monsters themselves.

How Harmful Are Hallucinogens?

❝It's not just the Bush administration that views psychedelics as harmful; since we were little we've been bombarded with myths and propaganda about the evils of their use, from the preaching of the nationwide D.A.R.E. program to widely circulated wives' tales.❞

—Genevieve Diesing, *Northern Star*.

❝Research in animals links MDMA exposure to long-term damage to neurons that are involved in mood, thinking, and judgment. A study in nonhuman primates showed that exposure to MDMA for only 4 days caused damage to serotonin nerve terminals that was evident 6 to 7 years later. While similar neurotoxicity has not been definitively shown in humans, the wealth of animal research indicating MDMA's damaging properties suggests that MDMA is not a safe drug for human consumption.❞

—National Institute on Drug Abuse, "InfoFacts: MDMA (ecstasy)."

The debate over the benefits and negative side effects of hallucinogens has been going on for decades. Proponents for the positive effects of hallucinogens argue that these drugs have been "demonized" and "mythologized" into something they are not. Some researchers contend that hallucinogenic drugs may have possible therapeutic effects. Others support the recreational use of these drugs as a way to connect to a higher power.

Many people, including doctors and researchers, argue that some hallucinogenic drugs should be legal for both medical and spiritual uses because no evidence proves that they are addictive or particularly harmful when used in controlled settings. They insist people should not be denied access to these drugs that can have long-lasting, positive spiritual effects.

However, opponents of hallucinogens point to some strong negative effects of these drugs, citing bad trips and even death. Accordingly, doctors and researchers point out that the potential benefits of hallucinogens have not held up to scientific scrutiny, and the medical and therapeutic benefits of these drugs are questionable.

> " **Proponents for the positive effects of hallucinogens argue that these drugs have been "demonized" and "mythologized" into something they are not.** "

Adding to the confusion in the debate is the subjective nature of individual responses to hallucinogens. Scientists have found that individuals' responses to the drugs vary. A 1960 study found that LSD responses may vary according to the personality of the research subjects. Some people reported positive experiences while others reported anxiety. Psychiatrist Rick Strassman of the University of New Mexico School of Medicine explains how these contradictions can occur:

> In the case of the psychedelics [hallucinogens], perhaps more so than for any other psychoactive drugs . . . set and setting play a crucial role in the subjective experience, as well as the objective interpretation, of drug effects. . . . *Set* in this context refers to the subject's expectations and mental and physical state. *Setting* partakes of both the physical and the psychological environment, including the expectation and behavior (set) of the research team.[10]

Therefore, outcomes of psychedelics depend much more on factors that influence therapeutic effectiveness than other, established medicines do, such as aspirin or Prozac. So, for many reasons hallucinogens remain a debatable topic in the scientific community and the culture in general.

How Can Hallucinogens Be Helpful?

Hallucinogens have been researched for decades for the treatment of both medical conditions and psychological disorders. Shortly after drugs like LSD were first synthesized, research began on their benefits for psychotherapy and as treatment for psychological disorders. After World War II, LSD was researched as a way to produce what doctors called a "controlled psychosis" that could help in the treatment of disorders like schizophrenia. Though research has been more difficult since hallucinogens were classified as Schedule I drugs, the possible benefits of these drugs continues to be explored.

> **Shortly after drugs like LSD were first synthesized, research began on their benefits for psychotherapy and as treatment for psychological disorders.**

Possible Treatment for Psychological Disorders and Addiction

Hallucinogenic drugs have been researched as possible aids in psychotherapy and treatments for alcoholism, autism, depression, and schizophrenia, to name a few. Researchers at the University of Arizona recently studied the use of psilocybin for the treatment of obsessive-compulsive disorder, and researchers in South Carolina are currently examining the use of MDMA (Ecstasy) as a treatment for post-traumatic stress disorder. According to scientist Torsten Passie, one doctor working on the positive effects of hallucinogenic drugs, "It seems that MDMA (Ecstasy) . . . can detraumatise people from experiences that have left them in a state of heavy tension and friction." Passie explains that to achieve success in using hallucinogens as therapeutic drugs "you first have to prepare a safe and stable therapeutic relationship with the patient so as to have a safe inner setting, and you need a safe external setting too,"[11] but he emphasizes that it is quite possible to establish an appropriate environment so the hallucinogenic drugs will benefit patients.

Although studies conducted in the 1960s on the use of LSD in the treatment of alcoholism have sometimes been viewed skeptically, recent research suggests that there may be some value in those studies. History of medicine professor Erika Dyck at the University of Alberta in Canada recently followed up with an initial 1962 study on LSD as a treatment for alcoholism published in *Quarterly Journal for Studies on Alcohol*. Dr. Dyck found that over 40 years later, many of the study participants reported positive experiences with the research, and some participants still had not had a single drink of alcohol in that 40 years.

Possible Benefits for the Terminally III

Research is also being conducted on how hallucinogenic drugs may benefit cancer patients. One study at the Harbor-UCLA Medical Center is researching how psilocybin may be used as a treatment for anxiety for patients who are in

> **Although studies conducted in the 1960s on the use of LSD in the treatment of alcoholism have sometimes been viewed skeptically, recent research suggests that there may be some value in those studies.**

the advanced stages of cancer. According to Ken Liska, author of *Drugs and the Human Body,* "LSD has been used in terminal cancer patients who experience persistent pain. These people get pain relief during the LSD therapy and afterward do not seem to mind the pain as much as before." MDMA, or Ecstasy, has also been used for the terminally ill. Liska notes that it brings about feelings of "peace, openness, insight, delight, [and] self-awareness."[12]

Are Hallucinogens Helpful Spiritually?

Just as hallucinogens have been used for thousands of years for spiritual and religious ceremonies, they continue to be used all over the world for similar purposes. In the Western Hemisphere, people in Oaxaca, Mexico, use hallucinogenic mushrooms for medicinal and spiritual healing. Southwestern Native American tribes use peyote in ceremonies where spiritual guidance is needed, and it is currently legal for members of the Native American Church to use peyote in their spiritual ceremonies. Any adult wishing to take part in the peyote ceremonies may do so, and the ceremonies are used to help make decisions that affect the tribal community, such as selecting leaders.

Supporters of the spiritual benefits of hallucinogenics contend that these drugs should be legal in wider circles and that the spiritual "trips" from the drugs can have positive, life-changing effects on people. These positive mystical and spiritual reactions to hallucinogens are described by Dr. Rick Strassman in the following passage:

> Mystical states of consciousness are characterized by profound alterations of one's sense of self, and in the experiences of time and space. Merging into a white light, a sense of timelessness within the eternal present, and a powerful interconnectedness of all existence are hallmarks of this state. In addition, powerful emotions are associated with these genitive and perceptual effects. There is the unshakeable conviction that consciousness is not dependent upon the body and, subsequently, that death is not the end of consciousness.[13]

With the current interest in discovering the biological basis of religious experience, hallucinogens would seem to be useful in the search.

What Are the Dangers of Hallucinogens?

In the 1960s hallucinogenic drugs like LSD went from promising therapeutic drugs to dangerous and illegal substances. Cases for and against LSD were made in the newspapers and on television. Even Congress got involved, conducting hearings on the recreational use of hallucinogenics. The government was concerned about the growing popularity of the drugs, and the media attention to the dangers of these drugs prompted Congress to act, making most hallucinogens illegal. As the drugs became more rejected by public officials, researchers like Albert Hofmann were dismayed. According to Hofmann, "They did not use it in the right way, and they did not have the right conditions. So they were not adequately prepared for it."[14]

In 1968 federal Drug Abuse Control Amendments were modified to make LSD illegal, along with other hallucinogenic drugs like mescaline and psilocybin. The U.S. Department of Health and Human Services claimed that hallucinogens can have negative effects on the brain, the heart, and one's "well-being" and "self-control."

But it is not just the U.S. government that has expressed concern about the negative effects of hallucinogens. Scientists have long been aware of the possible negative effects of hallucinogenic drugs. "Bad trips, "characterized by feelings of fear, paranoia, and panic, are a common negative side effect of drugs like LSD, mescaline, and psilocybin. Another possible dangerous side effect of hallucinogenic drug use is the occurrence of flashbacks. A flashback occurs when a person has an unexpected but very vivid reoccurrence of the experience of using the hallucinogenic drug. Flashbacks have also been described as very intense and very frightening daydreams. There are three types of flashbacks: emotional, somatic, and perceptual. Emotional flashbacks are the most dangerous and are similar to a bad trip. Emotional flashbacks bring about feelings of extreme panic and fear, and some people have hurt and even killed themselves during an emotional flashback. Somatic flashbacks bring about "altered body sensations," such as tremors, weakness, and dizziness. In perceptual flashbacks, users reexperience some of the visual or auditory elements of the original trip.

> " Bad flashbacks are more common in chronic users with personality disorders but sometimes occur in healthy people who have used hallucinogens only occasionally. "

Although the exact cause is uncertain, in some cases bad trips have caused users to fall into depression and experience continual flashbacks of a bad trip. Although flashbacks of "good" trips are often desired by users, flashbacks of bad trips can be traumatic, especially when they continue for long periods of time. Bad flashbacks are more common in chronic users with personality disorders but sometimes occur in healthy people who have used hallucinogens only occasionally.

Additionally, one of the biggest concerns with hallucinogens is the impaired judgment of users, which can lead to rash decisions and accidents. According to chemist Paul May at the University of Bristol in the United Kingdom:

Although LSD is relatively non-toxic and non-addictive, various governments around the world outlawed it after a number of fatal accidents were reported. Such accidents involved, for example, people under the influence of LSD jumping to their deaths off high buildings thinking they could fly. Research in the 60s and 70s showed that there was also a considerable psychological risk with the drug and that high doses, especially in inappropriate settings, often caused panic reactions. For individuals who have a low threshold for psychosis, a bad LSD trip could be the triggering event for the onset of full-blown psychosis.[15]

Although early researchers of hallucinogenic drugs like LSD reported very low rates of psychosis, two studies since the 1960s have reported psychosis in at least some patients using drugs like LSD. Moreover, new studies are also raising concerns about the long-term side effects of hallucinogenic drugs. One 1998 study on MDMA, or Ecstasy, from the National Institute of Mental Health found that habitual users of Ecstasy suffered from damaged serotonin-transmitting neurons in the brain even after they quit using Ecstasy. Researchers speculate that this effect is caused by the breakdown of too much neurotransmitter in the neurons, leaving by-products that are toxic and kill the neurons, resulting in severe depression.

> " Emotional addiction is a particular concern with MDMA because of its damaging effects on serotonin neurons. "

Are Hallucinogens Addictive?

While scientists may disagree on the benefits and costs of hallucinogenic drugs, most agree that they are not physically addictive. This means that users do not develop any kind of physical dependency on the drugs and do not experience withdrawal when not taking the drugs. Additionally, users report exhaustion after trips from hallucinogenic drugs and therefore are unlikely to use them frequently. However, the drugs may be emotionally addictive because users may "feel" dependent on them.

Emotional addiction is a particular concern with MDMA because of its damaging effects on serotonin neurons. However, users do not meet typical "addiction" criteria. MDMA users have been able to improve after use has ended without undergoing traditional treatment for addiction: instead, they are most helped by antidepressants that increase serotonin levels.

Can People Die from Using Hallucinogens?

In general, most doctors and scientists agree that hallucinogens are not directly life-threatening to users. No officially documented toxic fatalities have been associated with LSD use, but deaths have been reported from other hallucinogens, such as MDMA. These are primarily due to circulatory problems (for example, arrhythmias, which are abnormal muscle contractions in the heart). Although controlled use of hallucinogens may not be life threatening, deaths have been reported from bad trips where extreme panic and fear caused users to commit suicide. One example, are the reports of people trying to flee a bad trip by jumping out of a window. These concerns have led to the outlawing of hallucinogens in the United States and other countries.

Primary Source Quotes*

How Harmful Are Hallucinogens?

66 The main reason LSD is dangerous is because it's unpredictable in its effects. . . . The most dangerous thing that can happen is that someone has a complete break with reality and thinks they can fly or stop traffic. 99

—Jerry Frankenheim, quoted in Billy Cate, "Heads Up: Real News About Drugs and Your Body," *Scholastic Choices*, October 2003.

Frankenheim works for the National Institute on Drug Abuse's Division of Neuroscience and Behavioral Research.

66 The time certainly has come for a full appreciation of the beneficial uses that LSD has to offer. With renewed interest, it becomes necessary to understand better this chemical substance, its origins, effects, and dangers to guard against misuse and to allow for therapeutic and spiritual applications that are compatible with its uniquely characteristic actions. 99

—Michael Montagne, "From Problem Child to Wonder Child: LSD Turns 50," *Newsletter of the Multidisciplinary Association for Psychedelic Studies*, April 1993.

Montagne is professor of social pharmacy and acting associate dean of graduate studies at the Massachusetts College of Pharmacy and Health Sciences.

* Editor's Note: While the definition of a primary source can be narrowly or broadly defined, for the purposes of Compact Research, a primary source consists of: 1) results of original research presented by an organization or researcher; 2) eyewitness accounts of events, personal experience, or work experience; 3) first-person editorials offering pundits' opinions; 4) government officials presenting political plans and/or policies; 5) representatives of organizations presenting testimony or policy.

66 **If [psilocybin], if any drug, could help people with OCD, with mental illness, then we should explore it.** 99

—Francisco A. Moreno, "Researchers Explore New Visions for Hallucinogens," *Chronicle of Higher Education*, December 2006.

Moreno is a psychiatrist at the University of Arizona who had reported successfully treating difficult cases of obsessive-compulsive disorder with psilocybin.

66 **The most common danger of hallucinogen use is impaired judgment that leads to rash decisions and accidents.** 99

—U.S. Drug Enforcement Administration Web site, "Hallucinogens," 2007.

The U.S. Drug Enforcement Administration or DEA, is responsible for enforcing illegal-substance laws, including the growing, manufacturing, distribution, and trafficking of illegal substances. It was created in 1973 by President Richard Nixon to unify and coordinate the nation's drug combating efforts.

66 **The hippies believe that the mind has imprinted upon it memories of all ages past and possibly projections of the future as well. These prehistoric and archetypic perceptions are released, it is thought, by psychedelic experience.** 99

—Mardi J. Horowitz, "Flashbacks: Recurrent Intrusive Images After the Use of LSD," *American Journal of Psychiatry*, October 4, 1969.

Horowitz is currently director of the Center on Conscious and Unconscious Mental Processes and director of the Center on Stress and Personality at the University of California–San Francisco.

66 We don't know all their [mushrooms'] dark sides. I wouldn't in any way want to underestimate the potential risks. 99

—Roland Griffiths, quoted in Ron Winslow, "Go Ask Alice: Mushroom Drug Is Studied Anew," *Wall Street Journal*, July 11, 2006.

Griffiths is a professor of neuroscience, psychiatry, and behavioral biology at Johns Hopkins University.

66 The banning of psychedelics has been an absolute disaster for consciousness and medical research. 99

—Rick Doblin, quoted in Steven Kotler, "Drugs in Rehab," *Psychology Today*, March/April 2005.

Doblin founded MAPS (Multidisciplinary Association for Psychedelic Studies) in 1986. He is currently the head of the organization.

66 The whole taboo around recreational drug use can make the study of these drugs very difficult. We need to get a balance between these social taboos and what's best for patients. 99

—Richard Horton, "Psychedelics: Leading Medical Journal Calls for More LSD in Research Labs," *Drug War Chronicle*, April 2006.

Horton is the editor of the British medical journal *Lancet*.

66 Because of their profound effects, hallucinogens should be restricted to research use exclusively in a hospital setting. In our opinion, their use at this time for any other purpose or in any other setting is dangerous. 99

—Bernard Wilkens, Sidney Malitz, and Harold Esecover, "Clinical Observations of Simultaneous Hallucinogen Administration in Identical Twins," *American Journal of Psychiatry*, March 1962.

Wilkens, Malitz, and Esecover were researchers at the Department of Experimental Psychiatry at the New York State Psychiatric Institute when they published research in 1962 that involved administering LSD and psilocybin to identical twins.

66 The great value of LSD-25 lies in the fact that when the therapeutic situation is properly structured the patient can, and often does . . . develop a level of self-understanding and self-acceptance which may surpass that of the average normal person. 99

—D.B. Blewett and N. Chwelos, *Handbook for the Therapeutic Use of Lysergic Acid Diethylamide-25*, 1959.

Blewett and Chwelos were early researchers of the possible positive therapeutic effects of LSD. Their *Handbook for the Therapeutic Use of Lysergic Acid Diethylamide-25* was often used by therapists pioneering the use of LSD in therapy during the 1950s and 1960s.

66 Morphine works for pain, but it's horrendous when used in an addictive way. . . . The same may or may not be true for hallucinogens. 99

—Alan Leshner, "Scientists Test Hallucinogens for Mental Ills," *New York Times,* March 13, 2001.

Leshner was appointed director of the National Institute on Drug Abuse (NIDA) in 1994. NIDA supports the majority of the world's research on the health aspects of drug abuse and addiction.

66 You can safely and fairly reliably occasion a mystical experience using psilocybin that may lead to positive changes in a person. 99

—Roland R. Griffiths, quoted in Bruce Bower, "Chemical Enlightenment: Sign Up for the Scientific, Psychedelic Mystical Tour," *Science News,* September, 2006.

Griffiths is professor of behavioral biology and neuroscience and psychiatry at the Johns Hopkins University School of Medicine.

How Harmful Are Hallucinogens?

- The Hallucinogen Rating Scale (HRS) was developed in **1995** to help scientists measure the effects of psychedelic drugs on research subjects more objectively.

- Ergotamine, like LSD, a derivative of ergot, has been used for the treatment of **migraine** headaches for over 50 years.

- Ophthalmologists use atropine, one of the hallucinogens from belladonna, to dilate eyes during examinations.

- **Hyoscyamine**, another derivative of belladonna, is currently used to treat gastrointestinal disorders.

- In the early to mid-nineteenth century, scopolamine was given to women during childbirth to induce a "**twilight sleep**."

- Ergot poisoning has been a problem historically, with **40,000** deaths attributed to it during A.D. 944 alone.

- Because it causes deep amnesia and is easily found in many South American plants, scopolamine has been used by criminals in thefts and as a **date-rape** drug.

- The anticholinergic hallucinogens, if taken in sufficient amounts, have the same effect as **nerve gases** and so are potentially fatal.

Hallucinogens Are Among the Least Addictive Drugs

This chart reflects the clinicians' and researchers' subjective ratings of 12 drugs in terms of tolerance, withdrawal, and addiction. It shows that researchers agree that hallucinogenic drugs like LSD and MDMA (Ecstasy) are the least addictive of common drugs, even caffeine.

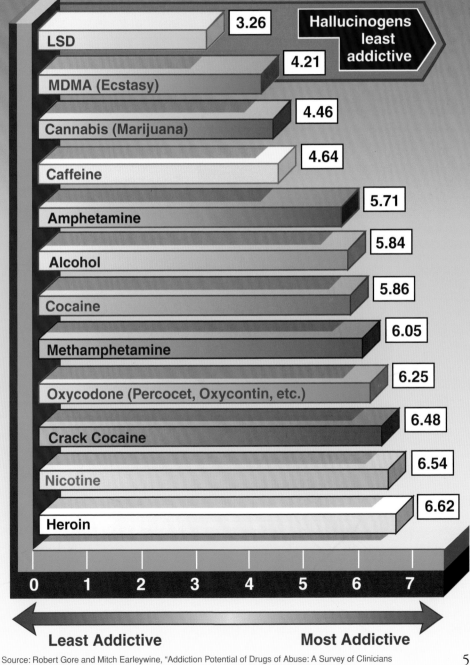

Least Addictive   Most Addictive

Source: Robert Gore and Mitch Earleywine, "Addiction Potential of Drugs of Abuse: A Survey of Clinicians and Researchers," Department of Psychology, University of Southern California, October 2004.

Ecstasy Users Aware of Some Risks

This chart reflects information from a recent survey of reported Ecstasy users. This survey was conducted by Erowid, an organization supporting nonjudgmental information on drugs. Erowid surveyed 923 Ecstasy users to judge their awareness of the risks of the drug. The survey indicated that well over half were quite aware that there are some risks associated with Ecstasy use.

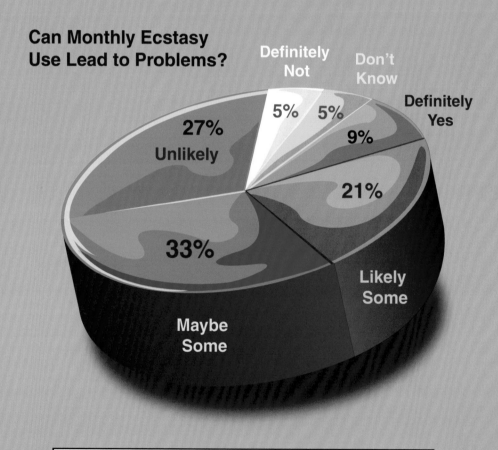

Can Monthly Ecstasy Use Lead to Problems?

- Definitely Not — 5%
- Don't Know — 5%
- Definitely Yes — 9%
- Likely Some — 21%
- Maybe Some — 33%
- Unlikely — 27%

Erowid survey of 923 reported Ecstasy users

Source: Erowid, "The Myth That Ecstasy Users Think Ecstasy Is Safe," an Erowid Web survey, November 2004.

- Lysergic acid diethylamide **(LSD)** is one of the most potent synthetic hallucinogens.

- LSD users may spend hours or even **days** recovering from the drug's effects.

- **"Rolling"** is a slang term used to describe being high on Ecstasy.

Students Sense of Risk Using LSD Once or Twice Declining

This graph reflects 30 years of student surveys on the risk associated with using LSD just once or twice. Since 1976, the percentage of students seeing "great risk" in using LSD once or twice has steadily declined.

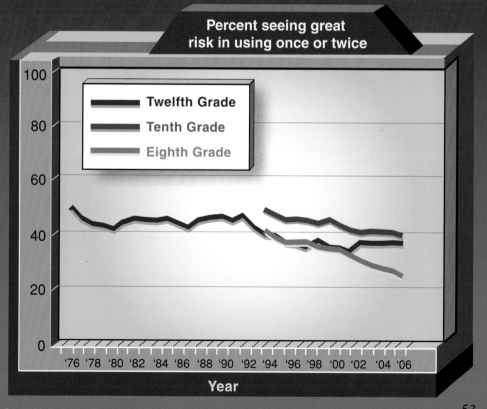

Percent seeing great risk in using once or twice

Number of Emergency Room Visits for Hallucinogen Users Is Small

This chart reflects national estimates of drug-related emergency room visits in 2004. This information was collected by the Drug Abuse Warning Network (DAWN), a division of the U.S. Department of Health and Human Services. Emergency rooms in the U.S. report a much smaller number of visits for hallucinogenic drugs when compared with other drugs.

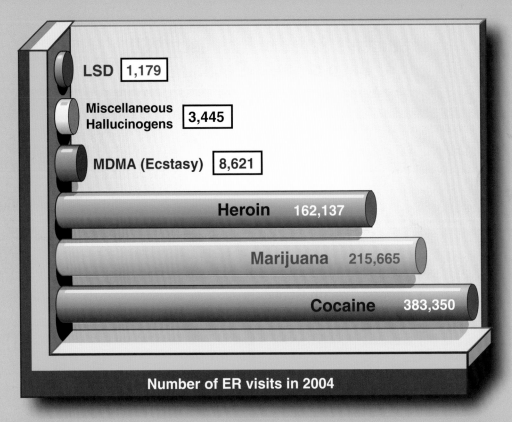

LSD 1,179

Miscellaneous Hallucinogens 3,445

MDMA (Ecstasy) 8,621

Heroin 162,137

Marijuana 215,665

Cocaine 383,350

Number of ER visits in 2004

Source: U.S. Department of Health and Human Services, Substance Abuse and Mental Health Services Administration, "Drug Abuse Warning Network, 2004: National Estimates of Drug-Related Emergency Room Visits," 2004. http://DAWNinfo.samhsa.gov.

How Serious a Problem Are Hallucinogens for Society?

66 **My overall experience of ecstasy at a rave was positive. I had a good time, enjoyed dancing and hanging out with my friends, and as a bonus worked through some work stress.** 99

—anonymous rave partygoer, The Vaults of Erowid.

66 **Some fatal accidents have . . . occurred among [LSD] users who could not perceive the reality of their situation. They hallucinate safe situations when they are actually in danger.** 99

—Brown University, "Health Education."

In the 1990s interest in hallucinogens began to rise, especially among the same demographic that had used them most frequently in the 1960s and 1970s, young men and women who were mainly from the middle class.

Although it is not clear why hallucinogenic drug use began to rise dramatically in the 1990s, a couple of hypotheses exist. First, some think that new research asserting that these drugs were not addictive and were not necessarily harmful replaced many of the myths about the dangers of these drugs. Certainly, drug use, even hallucinogenic drug use, is dangerous, but hallucinogens began to develop a reputation as a "safe" drug when compared to highly addictive drugs like crack and heroin. Second, some think that the rise in hallucinogenic drug use is simply a part of a greater pattern of increased drug use among Americans in the 1990s.

> **Certainly, drug use, even hallucinogenic drug use, is dangerous, but hallucinogens began to develop a reputation as a "safe" drug when compared to highly addictive drugs like crack and heroin.**

National surveys indicate that drug use in general was on the rise in the 1990s. Indeed, surveys from the late 1990s indicate that while the number of high school students who experimented with hallucinogens increased every year since 1990, the number of high school students who reported using a variety of drugs such as marijuana and cocaine also increased. Although surveys indicate that the number of students who tried hallucinogens leveled off in the early 2000s and there has been some decline, authorities remain concerned about the high number of adolescents who have experimented with hallucinogenic drugs.

Why Were Hallucinogens Made Illegal in Most Cases?

When hallucinogenic drugs became more readily available in the 1960s, people began to experiment with the drugs, and some drugs, such as LSD, became quite popular among certain groups. With this use, however, came some dangers. Because one of the biggest dangers of hallucinogenic drug use is the unusual way people may behave while on a trip, some people did hurt themselves and others while on these drugs. According to research in the *American Journal of Psychiatry*, after 1965 the number of problems associated with LSD use rose dramatically and has remained a problem:

> Since approximately the fall of 1965 the incidence of adverse LSD reactions throughout the country has mushroomed. At the UCLA Neuropsychiatric Institute prior to September 1965 one problem case associated with LSD ingestion was seen approximately every two months. Beginning at that time the incidence increased gradually from five to 20 cases a month, with three to

five telephone calls being received, for every person seen, from other persons in trouble from LSD who were not subsequently seen. Other hospitals throughout the country have reported a similar increase. . . . These patients came most often with hallucinations, followed by anxiety to the point of panic, by depression, often with suicidal thoughts or attempts, and by confusion.[16]

The Drug Enforcement Administration considers hallucinogenic drugs dangerous because of the possibility of accidental harm while using these drugs. Some government officials have also mentioned that hallucinogenic drugs are possible "gateway" drugs, meaning that people who experiment with these drugs are more likely to move on to more dangerous and addictive drugs. These assertions remain unproven, however, as does the idea that there are no accepted medical uses of these drugs.

While hallucinogenic drug use increased dramatically throughout the 1990s, the number of emergency room visits associated with these drugs did not increase. According to the U.S. Department of Justice, "Although . . . surveys show increases in hallucinogen use, particularly among the young, data from emergency rooms (ERs) across the country do not. The percentages of ER mentions for LSD or PCP in the Drug Abuse Warning Network (DAWN) are low (fewer than 0.01 percent)"[17]

However, the U.S. Department of Justice is also quick to point out that surveys indicate hallucinogen users are using these drugs at lower potency levels than in the 1960s and 70s. According to Dana Hunt, researcher for the U.S. Department of Justice, emergency rooms are not seeing the "acute incidents requiring emergency medical attention"[18] that were seen in the past. But the same surveys indicate that hallucinogen users are using the drug more frequently in these smaller amounts, and while this trend may not produce a high number of emergency room situations, such frequent use of hallucinogens can have long-lasting negative effects. According to the National Institute on Drug Abuse, people who use hallucinogenic drugs like LSD can quickly develop a short-lived tolerance to the drugs. This means users would need to increase the amount of the "hit" in order to feel the same effects as a smaller hit before. But this tolerance does not last long and is lost if the user quits taking the drug for even just a few days. Thus, danger of overdose can arise if the user does not take this loss of tolerance into account when he or she resumes using the drug.

Why Are Some Hallucinogens Still Legal?

Some people, such as members of MAPS, the Multidisciplinary Association of Psychedelic Studies, have argued for decades that it is absurd that nonaddictive drugs like hallucinogens are illegal when an addictive drug like alcohol remains legal. They contend that hallucinogens are relatively safe and that more research needs to be done to explore the possible benefits of these drugs. And the reality is that the U.S. government has allowed these drugs to remain legal in certain situations. Peyote is still a legal part of the religious ceremonies of the Native American Church, a group that consists of hundreds of thousands of members in North America. The following passage describes how this group uses peyote in their ceremonies:

> " The reality is that the U.S. government has allowed these drugs to remain legal in certain situations. "

> Native American Church "meetings" begin after dark, often in tipis. The meetings take place around a fire, last all night, and include a great deal of singing, chanting, and praying, all coordinated by a leader, or "road man." Peyote is eaten throughout the night, and participants ask the spirit of the cactus to help make them better people, better able to deal with their problems. Sometimes the ritual includes elements of Christian worship. Church members tell many stories of cures of illness resulting from peyote meetings, as well as cures of alcoholism, an addiction notoriously resistant to treatment by conventional means.[19]

Although this legal use of a hallucinogen remains controversial, and some states have limited this use to members of Native American tribes only, the Native American Church and other religious groups have fought and won many court battles to keep hallucinogens a part of their ceremonies. A 1993 federal bill called the Religious Freedom Restoration Act, which afforded more protections for religious freedoms, seems to have provided greater protection for religious groups who seek to use hallucinogens as a part of their ceremonies. In fact, as recently as 2006 the Supreme Court ruled unanimously that a congregation in New Mexico, which has roots in South America, can use a hallucinogenic tea containing DMT as a part of a four-hour ritual meant to help the group connect with God. While the Justice Department asserted that DMT is an unsafe drug and was banned under the Controlled Substances Act, the Supreme Court ruled that the U.S. government could not limit the group's religious freedom.

> " A 1993 federal bill called the Religious Freedom Restoration Act, which afforded more protections for religious freedoms, seems to have provided greater protection for religious groups who seek to use hallucinogens as a part of their ceremonies. "

Evaluating the Impact of the Traffic in Illegal Hallucinogens

There are many ways illegal drug use can affect our society, including the effects of the drugs themselves on users and the cost of the drugs to users that may lead to violent or criminal situations. According to researchers, three types of violence are associated with drugs: pharmacologic crime, directly related to the drugs' effects on the users; economic crime, related to the drugs' costs to users; and systemic crime, related to the trafficking of drugs.

For the most part, as of the late 1990s hallucinogens had not been linked to high pharmacologic crime. There also seems to be very little economic crime associated with hallucinogens because they are quite inexpensive, costing between one dollar and five dollars per dose, and their use is highest among middle- and upper-class young people who have access to plenty of money and would not need to resort to crime to obtain funds to buy the drugs. Finally, systemic crime has not been found to be a significant is-

> **Although illicit drug use and violent crime go hand in hand, the general assumption is that the crime connected with hallucinogenic drugs does not seem to be nearly as high as it is with other Schedule I drugs, such as heroin.**

sue with hallucinogenic drugs, as it has been with drugs like heroin and cocaine. Only a handful of chemists and major distributors have been around since the 1960s and 70s, and any local production of hallucinogenic drugs seems to stay local and does not interfere with the major suppliers and traffickers. Although illicit drug use and violent crime go hand in hand, the general assumption is that the crime connected with hallucinogenic drugs does not seem to be nearly as high as it is with other Schedule I drugs, such as heroin.

However, this is not to say that no crime is connected with hallucinogenic drugs. When gangs have been involved with hallucinogenic drug production and trafficking systemic crime has occurred.

Raves

Hallucinogenic drugs are sometimes used at raves to reinforce the trance-like state of ravegoers that the music and lights create. Although raves have declined somewhat in recent years, they are still considered quite popular in some parts of the country, particularly the Midwest. Although many who attend these parties emphasize that they are not all about drugs but are more about enjoying the music and the sense of community, hallucinogenic drug use is so common that they have become associated with raves.

While organizations like the Multidisciplinary Association for Psychedelic Studies and researchers from many countries continue to call for a reclassification or legalization of hallucinogenic drugs, the U.S. government has made no steps in this direction. While the United States continues to grant a few permissions each year to scientists researching these Schedule I drugs, the number of research studies in the United States remains small, and restrictions remain tight. The dangers of these drugs are continually cited by government organizations.

How Serious a Problem Are Hallucinogens for Society?

66When I'm on LSD ..., it takes me to another world and into anther brain state where I've stopped thinking and started knowing.99

—Kevin Herbert, "LSD: The Geeks Wonder Drug?" *Wired*, January 16, 2006.

Herbert was one of the early employees of Cisco Systems, a computer technology company.

66A lot of people are doing drugs, but it's a very nonviolent crowd. I've worked a lot of raves, but only a handful of times have I seen any problems.99

—Michael Moss, "Organized Chaos," *Daily Camera Online*, June 30, 1995.

Moss, a rave club owner in Boulder, Colorado, commented on the drug use but emphasized the nonviolent nature of raves in an interview for the *Daily Camera*, a Boulder newspaper.

* Editor's Note: While the definition of a primary source can be narrowly or broadly defined, for the purposes of Compact Research, a primary source consists of: 1) results of original research presented by an organization or researcher; 2) eyewitness accounts of events, personal experience, or work experience; 3) first-person editorials offering pundits' opinions; 4) government officials presenting political plans and/or policies; 5) representatives of organizations presenting testimony or policy.

66 The peyote exception . . . has been in place since the outset of the Controlled Substances Act, and there is no evidence that it has 'undercut' the Government's ability to enforce the ban on peyote use by non-Indians. 99

—John Roberts, opinion of the Court, *Alberto R. Gonzales. Attorney General v. O Centro Espirita Beneficente Uniao Do Vegetal*, February 26, 2006.

Roberts was appointed chief justice of the U.S. Supreme Court in September 2005.

66 Most students said psychedelics don't interfere with schoolwork since they're reserved for special occasions. 99

—Jen Lennon, "Hallucinogens Have a Small but Loyal Local Following," *Athens News*, January 25, 2006.

Lennon is the Ohio University campus reporter to the *Athens News*, a local newspaper in Athens, Ohio. She interviewed many students on the Ohio University campus on the popularity of hallucinogenic drug use at the university.

66 There can be no doubt . . . that in the history of psychedelic drug use, lives have been lost, and minds permanently altered. 99

—Eugene Taylor, "Psychedelics," *Psychology Today*, July/August 1996.

Taylor is a lecturer in psychiatry at the Harvard Medical School, the vice president of the Swedenborg Chapel's Cambridge Society, executive faculty member at Saybrook Graduate School, senior psychologist with the psychiatry service at Massachusetts General Hospital, and an author.

"Users may think that ecstasy is fun and that it feels fairly harmless at the time. However, our results show slight but measurable impairments to memory as a result of use."

—Jacqui Rodgers, "Ecstasy Affects Memory, New International Study Shows," 2004. Eurekalert.org.

Rodgers is a lecturer in clinical psychology and senior academic tutor at the University of Newcastle in Australia where she oversees and evaluates the academic curriculum of the Newcastle Department of Clinical Psychology.

"Is [ecstasy] addictive? We simply don't know for sure."

—Howard Markel, "Ecstasy," Medscape, *WebMD*, 2004.

Markel is the George E. Wantz Distinguished Professor of the History of Medicine, professor of pediatrics and communicable diseases, and director of the Center for the History of Medicine at the University of Michigan.

"The plain fact is that the statistical evidence of the long-term effects of . . . hallucinogens on body and mental health is too slight to warrant generalization, and what there is does not support the view that they are in any way adverse. As distinct from narcotics, they are not addictive. No one has alleged, either, that hallucinogens can be significantly associated with physical defects."

—E. J. Mishan, *Pornography, Psychedelics & Technology: Essays on the Limits to Freedom*, 1980.

Mishan taught at the London School of Economics from 1956 to 1977.

66Other drugs, mostly hallucinogens, should be decriminalized but studied honestly, without researchers bent on finding reasons to make them illegal.**99**

—Clifford Thornton Jr., quoted in Tobin A. Coleman, "Green Party Candidate Stares Down the Odds," *Stamford (CT) Advocate*, May 29, 2006.

Thornton ran as the Green Party candidate in the 2006 gubernatorial race in Connecticut.

66The use of [the peyote] 'sacrament' is contained within the community. Any other use of this would not be a correct use of 'medicine.'**99**

—Native American Church of Strawberry Plains, Tennessee, "Statement on Peyote," n.d.

The Native American Church, also called Peyotism, originated in Oklahoma and involves the use of peyote.

66The worst consequence of spreading misinformation is that it steals time and energy from the true job—making sure qualified researchers have access and permission to investigate the real problems associated with hallucinogens.**99**

—Cheryl Pellerin, *Trips: How Hallucinogens Work in Your Brain*, 1998.

Pellerin is an independent science writer for broadcast and print media.

66Every few years, apparently, younger people believe it's not dangerous anymore and believe that the risks, if there are any, can be borne. The risks of let's say cocaine, heroin and hallucinogens and marijuana are different kinds of risks; but there are real risks associated with all of them.**99**

—William "Bill" Jefferson Clinton, interview with MTV, 1996.

Clinton was the forty-second president of the United States and served from 1993 to 2001.

Facts and Illustrations

How Serious a Problem Are Hallucinogens for Society?

- Many times **Ecstasy** is not pure and may be adulterated with additional drugs such as mescaline, methamphetamine, codeine, dextromethorphan (DXM), and/or parametnoxyamphetamine (PMA), which in turn can cause overdose and death.

- Johns Hopkins University researchers found that after just **four** days of use of the drug Ecstasy, effects were experienced up to **seven** years later.

- LSD users with a family history of **mental illness** run the risk of triggering long-term psychological illnesses.

- LSD is usually sold as a liquid, often packaged in small bottles designed to hold breath freshening drops, or on blotter paper, in **sugar cubes**, or gelatin squares. It is also sometimes sold as tablets.

- Survey data reported in the National Household Survey on Drug Abuse indicates that approximately **20.2 million** U.S. residents over the age of 12 have used LSD at least once in their lives.

- The occurrence of flashbacks was officially named in 2003 as "Hallucinogen Persisting Perception Disorder." Diagnosis requires the occurrence of disabling **flashbacks** after using hallucinogenic drugs without having used other drugs or being diagnosed with a psychiatric illness.

Hallucinogen Use by College Students and Young Adults Declines

This table shows the percentages of college students and young adults in 2004 and 2005 who reported using hallucinogens in the past month, the past year, and in their lifetimes. The percentages dropped slightly in all categories from 2004 to 2005.

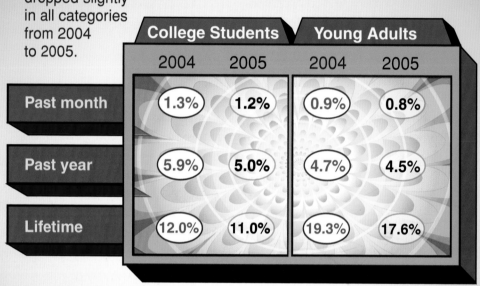

	College Students		Young Adults	
	2004	2005	2004	2005
Past month	1.3%	1.2%	0.9%	0.8%
Past year	5.9%	5.0%	4.7%	4.5%
Lifetime	12.0%	11.0%	19.3%	17.6%

Source: Office of National Drug Control Policy, "Drug Facts: Hallucinogens." www.whitehousedrugpolicy.gov.

- The visual effects of a trip on hallucinogens include the appearance of brightly colored, rapidly swirling and crawling **geometric patterns** that seem to appear in space, whether the user's eyes are open or not.

- The empathy for others that is often mentioned in trips on hallucinogenic drugs can become overwhelming, but the user may also lose all empathy for others and become quite self-absorbed.

- The most common names for LSD are acid, boomers, and yellow sunshine. Street terms for LSD are battery acid, dots, **Elvis**, Superman, and Lucy in the Sky with Diamonds.

- The common names for MDMA are Ecstasy, Adam, and **XTC**. Street names include Cristal, E, Eve, Hug Drug, Love Drug, and X.

- The National Drug Intelligence Center (NDIC) has noted that ecstasy is being dangerously combined with other drugs, such as marijuana and heroin, at raves.

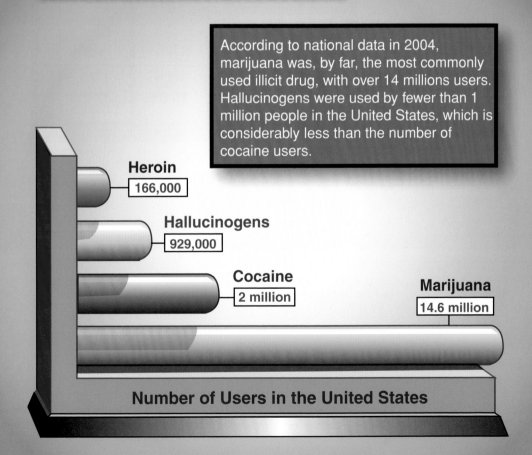

Which Drugs Do People Use?

According to national data in 2004, marijuana was, by far, the most commonly used illicit drug, with over 14 millions users. Hallucinogens were used by fewer than 1 million people in the United States, which is considerably less than the number of cocaine users.

Heroin
166,000

Hallucinogens
929,000

Cocaine
2 million

Marijuana
14.6 million

Number of Users in the United States

Source: Office of National Drug Control Policy, "National Survey on Drug Use and Health: National Findings," 2005. www.whitehousedrugpolicy.gov.

Prisoners' Use of Hallucinogens

According to data from the Bureau of Justice Statistics, approximately 32.9 percent of state prisoners and 25.9 percent of federal prisoners surveyed in 2004 indicated that they used hallucinogens at some point in their lives.

	State Prisoners		Federal Prisoners	
	1997	2004	1997	2004
At time of offense	1.8%	2.0%	0.8%	1.9%
In month before offense	4.0%	5.9%	1.7%	5.8%
Regularly*	11.3%	13.3%	6.4%	11.9%
Ever in lifetime	28.7%	32.9%	19.0%	25.9%

*Used drugs at least once a week for at least a month.

Source: Office of National Drug Control Policy, "Drug Facts: Hallucinogens." www.whitehousedrugpolicy.gov.

- A study in Denver, Colorado, confirms that while driving under the influence of hallucinogens like LSD is dangerous, it is also rare. Of **242** drivers who were detained for "driving while impaired" between 1988 and 1990, only one case of LSD was confirmed.

- **"Fry"** is a slang term for marijuana or tobacco cigarettes that have been dipped in PCP and then dried. Sometimes, users are unaware that marijuana they purchased has been dipped in PCP.

How Can Illegal Hallucinogens Be Controlled?

66 Adults seeking solace or insight ought to be allowed to consume psychedelics such as LSD, psilocybin, and mescaline. U.S. laws now classify them as Schedule 1 drugs, banned for all purposes because of their health risks. But recent studies have shown that psychedelics—which more than 20 million Americans have ingested—can be harmless and even beneficial when taken under appropriate circumstances. 99

—John Horgan, "Tripping De-Light Fantastic: Are Psychedelic Drugs Good for You?"

66 When I mentioned . . . that our federal (and many state) drug laws were irrational, I was immediately greeted with the demand that we solve the problem by legalizing drugs. If only things were so simple. The central problem with legalizing drugs is that it will increase drug consumption under almost any reasonable guess as to what the legalization (or more modestly, the decriminalization) regime would look like. 99

—James Q. Wilson, "Legalizing Drugs Makes Matters Worse."

The legalization of many hallucinogenic drugs remains controversial. When doctors and scientists as well as experienced users claim so frequently in the media that these drugs are not dangerous and can, in fact, be quite beneficial to people, it is easy to see why use is common and difficult to control.

While most hallucinogenic drugs remain tightly controlled, a growing number of Americans do not think the Schedule I classification for these drugs makes sense. Some, like E.J. Mishan, former professor at the London School of Economics, argue that many of the dangers surrounding these drugs, such as high dosages and impure drugs, could be eliminated if the drugs were legal. In fact, government regulations would make these drugs even safer than they are now. An author who has researched the impact of the legalization of drugs, Richard B. Karel, has written about the legalization of hallucinogenic drugs like LSD and MDMA. He and others argue that the costs of keeping such drugs illegal are far greater than the costs of legalization. He writes about how hallucinogens could be regulated to eliminate safety issues for those who would be likely to experience problems with the drugs:

> Because these drugs have positive potential when properly used, but are dangerous to a very small percentage of psychologically unstable individuals, the legal provision of such drugs would be conditioned on demonstration of knowledge as to their effects (Krippner, 1985; Kurland, 1985; Yensen, 1985; Wolfson, 1986). This could involve completion of a written examination, screening test, and interview. Cultivation of psilocybin, peyote cacti, or other psychedelic plants for personal use would be permitted.[20]

> **Despite the growing push to legalize hallucinogens or, at the very least, reclassify them, hallucinogens remain illegal substances and are considered quite dangerous by federal officials when used in uncontrolled settings.**

What Are Nonlegal Methods of Control?

Despite the growing push to legalize hallucinogens or, at the very least, reclassify them, hallucinogens remain illegal substances and are considered quite dangerous by federal officials when used in uncontrolled settings. Therefore, as the use of illicit drugs like hallucinogens has risen dramatically among teenagers and college students, the government and other agencies have worked hard to develop strong education campaigns that emphasize the dangers of these drugs.

The White House Office of National Drug Control Policy, established by the Anti-Drug Abuse Act of 1988, produces the annual National Drug Control Policy, which comes from the office of the president. The three main goals of the 2006 National Drug Control Policy were to stop drug abuse before it starts with national education and community programs, help America's drug users seek treatment, and disrupt current drug markets. One part of the 2006 policy was to devote $79.2 million to the Drug Free Communities (DFC) program. According to the White House Office of National Drug Control Policy's Web site, this program focuses on bringing together "community leaders and professionals in health care, law enforcement, and education to provide local, grassroots solutions to the challenges drug and alcohol abuse pose to their neighborhoods." Currently, the federal government has funded over 700 DFC coalitions. These coalitions exist in every state, and the government guarantees funding of up to $100,000 per year for 5 years to "develop a comprehensive community plan to address substance abuse problems."[21]

The government funds several efforts specifically to educate teenagers about the dangers of drug abuse and social pressures they may encounter. One of these programs is called Above the Influence. This program began in 2005 and features television and print advertisements as well as a Web-based campaign. This program attempts not only to educate teens but also to speak to them about the pressures to use and the rewards of resisting illegal drugs.

Student drug testing is also an important part of the government's drug control strategy. Basically, students who participate in school activities agree to be tested randomly for drugs and alcohol. Parental permission is required. The program has spread rapidly throughout the nation in the last decade or so. According to official reports from the White House:

> The program has demonstrated its effectiveness. Since the 2000 school year, the percentage of students testing positive for alcohol and other drugs has declined steadily. It's My Call/It's Our Call is designed to be therapeutic rather

than punitive. Students who test positive are invited to be evaluated and treated for addiction problems at the school system's expense. If students agree to evaluations and treatment, their positive results are not reported to school officials.[22]

Controlling Illegal Hallucinogens

Although law enforcement is a big part of preventing any kind of illegal drug use, research indicates that law enforcement officials struggle to control even the most dangerous drug-related crime, and since hallucinogen use and distribution does not create as many problems as drugs like crack cocaine, hallucinogenic drug use is often not a major priority. Still, state and local agencies work to educate their officers about the dangers and signs of hallucinogenic drug use. Others also work undercover to monitor "raves" where hallucinogenic drug use is so common.

Moreover, although hallucinogenic drugs received little attention in the President's National Drug Control Strategy, efforts to reduce the trafficking of MDMA, or Ecstasy, are mentioned in the president's current plan. According to data presented in the 2006 plan, MDMA seizures peaked in 2001 with a record number of domestic seizures of 11 million tablets. When intelligence revealed that large quantities of MDMA used in the United States at that time were coming primarily from labs in the Netherlands, federal agents in both the United States and the Netherlands worked to stop this illegal trafficking. According to recent reports, domestic seizures of MDMA tablets dropped to below 3 million tablets in the last 2 years.

> It is still important to remember that research indicates the best way to prevent drug use among teens is for parents to talk to their children about drugs early and often.

With this in mind, it is still important to remember that research indicates the best way to prevent drug use among teens is for parents to talk to their children about drugs early and often. According to the U.S. Department of Health and Human Services, "Teens who learn a lot about the risks of drugs from their parents are up to 54 percent less likely to try drugs."[23] To help educate parents on how to talk with their children and what to look for if they suspect their child might be using drugs, the U.S. Department of Health and Human Services provides free brochures and videos. The popular media has also worked to educate parents about hallucinogens by publishing guides to the slang associated with raves and hallucinogenic drug use to help parents know more about what their children are doing. Although teens have responded to such efforts by working to keep the slang just ahead of the publications, these efforts do seem to have helped parents and perhaps have been an important part of the effort to cut down on hallucinogenic drug use by teens, as raves and hallucinogenic drug use at raves have not continued to climb at the alarming rate witnessed during the 1990s.

Primary Source Quotes*

How Can Illegal Hallucinogens Be Controlled?

66 **Hallucinogen trafficking and abuse pose only a moderate threat to the United States because of limited availability.** 99

—U.S. Department of Justice, National Drug Intelligence Center, *National Drug Threat Assessment 2004*.

The National Drug Intelligence Center's mission is to give intelligence to national policy makers and law enforcement as well as support the intelligence community's antidrug efforts.

66 **People on hallucinogenic drugs are often difficult to communicate with and are unresponsive to reasonable requests, which makes our job as law enforcement officers very difficult.** 99

—David Trail, interview with the author, 2007.

Trail worked in law enforcement for 30 years, with 27 years of service as a campus safety officer at a small university outside of Dallas, Texas.

* Editor's Note: While the definition of a primary source can be narrowly or broadly defined, for the purposes of Compact Research, a primary source consists of: 1) results of original research presented by an organization or researcher; 2) eyewitness accounts of events, personal experience, or work experience; 3) first-person editorials offering pundits' opinions; 4) government officials presenting political plans and/or policies; 5) representatives of organizations presenting testimony or policy.

Primary Source Quotes

66 **Drug legalization and permissive drug policies will lead to a greater availability of dangerous drugs in our communities and undermine each nation's commitment to law enforcement, health care, education, commerce and the family.** 99

—The Drug Free America Foundation, "Mission Statement," 2007.

The Drug Free America Foundation, a nongovernmental organization, is a drug prevention and policy organization committed to developing, promoting, and sustaining global strategies, policies, and laws that will reduce illegal drug use, drug addiction, and drug-related injury and death.

66 **Many of the problems the drug war purports to resolve are in fact caused by the drug war itself. So-called "drug-related" crime is a direct result of drug prohibition's distortion of immutable laws of supply and demand.** 99

—Drug Policy Alliance, "What's Wrong with the Drug War?" 2007.

The Drug Policy Alliance is the leading organization in the United States promoting alternatives to the war on drugs.

66 **The drug war has failed—we spend nearly $50 billion annually on the drug war and problems related to drug abuse continue to worsen.** 99

—Ralph Nader, quoted in Adam Sparks, "Ralph Nader, the Leftist Conservative," SFGate.com, March 8, 2004.

Nader is an attorney and political activist.

❝I'm opposed to legalization because it is likely to increase the proportion of our population, in particular, our young people, using drugs. The drugs that are by far the most widely used are alcohol and tobacco. It is not a coincidence that those are legal drugs.❞

—Lloyd Johnston, "Monitoring the Future Head Researcher Speaks Out on Drug Trends, Drug War, Drug Policy," *Drug War Chronicle.* http://stopthedrugwar.org.

Johnston is research professor and distinguished research scientist at the University of Michigan's Institute for Social Research.

❝The bottom line is that parents are the most important people to eradicate the use of drugs by kids.❞

—Gary L. Somdahl, *Drugs and Kids: How Parents Can Keep Them Apart,* 1996.

Somdahl is a licensed youth chemical dependency counselor with the Carondelet Behavioral Health Center of Pasco, Washington.

❝While LSD use is widely acknowledged by teenagers, it generally goes undetected in a community until arrests bring it to the attention of the news media.❞

—Cynthia Favret, "An LSD Distribution Network," quoted in Leigh A. Henderson and William J. Glass, *LSD: Still with Us After All These Years,* 1994.

Favret is a clinical psychologist and author.

❝There are those who would 'solve' the drug problem by legalization of prohibited drugs, a solution that makes as much sense as solving the problem of bank robberies by legalizing that prohibited behavior.❞

—Robert L. DuPont, "Violence and Drugs," *Journal of Psychoactive Drugs,* October–December, 1997.

DuPont is a former director of the National Institute on Drug Abuse and worked as the "drug czar" for the United States as director of the Office of National Drug Control Policy.

"In terms of crime rates, the most serious mistake America ever made was to limit its repeal of Prohibition to a single drug—alcohol, the only drug that commonly triggers violent propensities in its users. Had we fully repealed drug prohibition in 1933, our crime rates today would be no more than half what they now are."

—Steven B. Duke. "How Drug Legalization Would Cut Crime," *Los Angeles Times*, 1993.

Duke is a Yale law professor and the coauthor, with Albert C. Gross, of *America's Longest War: Rethinking Our Tragic Crusade Against Drugs.*

"The legality of drugs often isn't relevant to their potential to do harm. Decisions are political rather than biological. If this weren't so, LSD would be legal but nicotine wouldn't be."

—Rebecca Walker-Sands, 2007 interview with the author.

Walker-Sands is a professor of psychology at Central Oregon Community College and teaches psychology courses at the University of Oregon.

"Creating real alternatives for those whose circumstances make them most vulnerable to drugs is crucial if we are to build on the progress we have already made in changing public attitudes toward drugs."

—Mathea Falco, *The Making of a Drug-Free America: Programs That Work*, 1992.

Falco has served as chief counsel of the Senate Judiciary Subcommittee on Juvenile Delinquency and as a special assistant to the president of the Drug Abuse Council.

❝The most effective policy really does start at the local level. The most local of all levels, by the way, is in somebody's home, where a mom or dad works with the children to help them make the right decisions.❞

—George W. Bush, speech given to the Vienna/Madison Community Antidrug Coalition in Vienna, Virginia, 2001.

George W. Bush is the forty-third President of the United States.

How Can Illegal Hallucinogens Be Controlled?

- The effects of MDMA include **increased heart rate** and blood pressure, so people with circulatory problems or heart disease face particular risk when using the drug.

- MDMA is typically sold as a tablet with logos like **smiley** faces, **clover** leaves, or **cartoon** characters.

- Psilocybin mushrooms are **ingested orally** and may be brewed as a tea or added to other foods to mask the bitter flavor of the mushrooms.

- The most common names for psilocybin are **magic** mushroom, mushroom, and shrooms. Street terms for psilocybin include Little Smoke, Mexican Mushrooms (because of the regions where they are most commonly found), and Silly Putty.

- To get around federal laws that have banned most hallucinogens, listing them as Schedule I substances, labs have produced "**generic**" versions of these drugs. While these new drugs are not specifically listed under the Controlled Substances Act, federal laws have had to be reformed to include these newly created copies.

- While surveys indicate that a high number of teens have used hallucinogenic drugs, the fact is that most teens do not use these drugs or drugs of any kind. The vast **majority** of teens have never even tried a hallucinogen.

Federal Government Spends Billions on Drug Abuse Treatment and Prevention

According to the president's National Drug Control Strategy, the federal government spends billions of dollars each year on drug abuse treatment and prevention designed to reduce the demand for drugs.

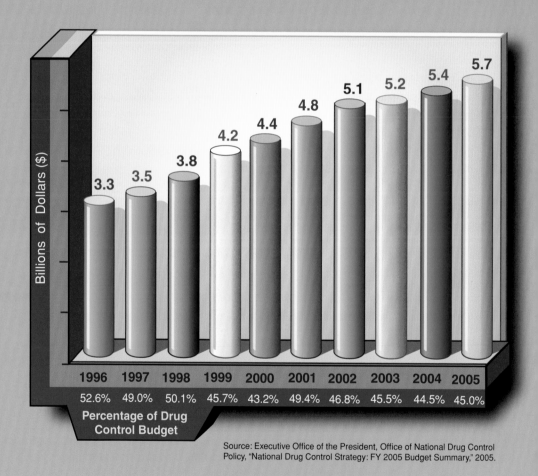

	1996	1997	1998	1999	2000	2001	2002	2003	2004	2005
Billions of Dollars ($)	3.3	3.5	3.8	4.2	4.4	4.8	5.1	5.2	5.4	5.7
Percentage of Drug Control Budget	52.6%	49.0%	50.1%	45.7%	43.2%	49.4%	46.8%	45.5%	44.5%	45.0%

Source: Executive Office of the President, Office of National Drug Control Policy, "National Drug Control Strategy: FY 2005 Budget Summary," 2005.

- While some Web sites list **PCP** as a hallucinogenic drug, most scientists now no longer consider PCP a hallucinogen because it affects the brain differently.

Many Americans Have Poor Opinion of the War on Drugs

According to a 2005 survey conducted by publicagenda.com, 50 percent of Americans gave the United States a grade of "D" or "F" for reducing illegal drug trafficking from other countries into the United States.

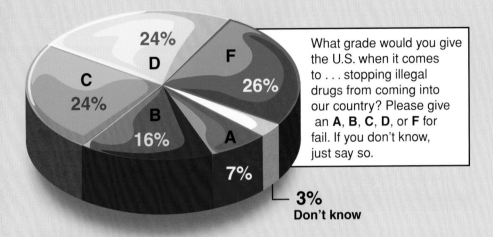

What grade would you give the U.S. when it comes to . . . stopping illegal drugs from coming into our country? Please give an **A**, **B**, **C**, **D**, or **F** for fail. If you don't know, just say so.

3%
Don't know

Source: Public Agenda, "Illegal Drugs: People's Chief Concerns," 2005. www.publicagenda.org.

Nearly Half of Americans Think the United States Is Losing Ground When It Comes to Illegal Drugs

According to 2005 surveys from the Pew Research Center, nearly 50 percent of Americans feel the United States is "losing ground" when it comes to the struggle against illegal drugs. Only 14 percent think the United States is making progress.

Do you think the problem of illegal drugs is about the same as it has been, that the country is making progress in this area, or that the country is losing ground?

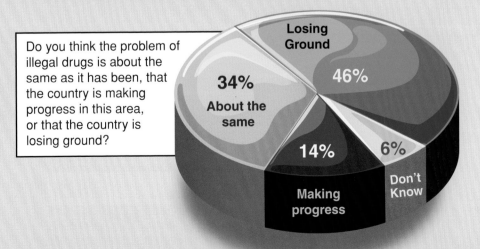

81

Source: Pew Research Center, "Illegal Drugs: People's Chief Concerns," 2005. www.publicagenda.org.

Americans See Drugs as a Serious Problem

Surveys indicate that over 70 percent of Americans feel drugs are a very serious problem in this country. However, only 30 percent feel that drugs are a very serious problem in the areas in which they live. These data indicate that while Americans perceive the drug problem as serious, most do not feel it is an issue in their neighborhoods.

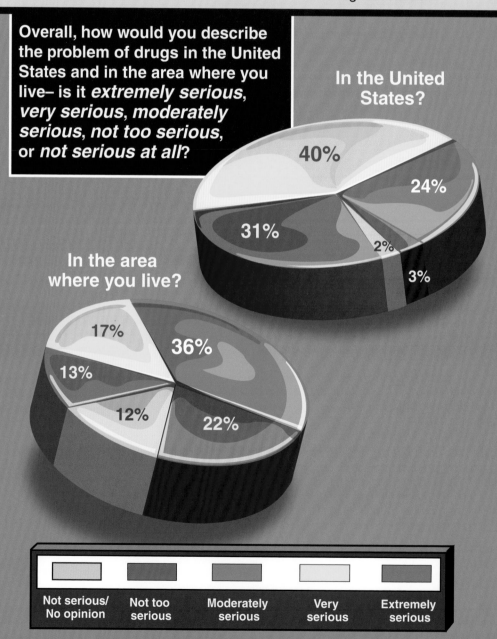

Overall, how would you describe the problem of drugs in the United States and in the area where you live— is it *extremely serious, very serious, moderately serious, not too serious,* or *not serious at all*?

In the United States?

40%
24%
31%
2%
3%

In the area where you live?

17%
36%
13%
12%
22%

Not serious/ No opinion | Not too serious | Moderately serious | Very serious | Extremely serious

Source: Gallup Poll, "Illegal Drugs: People's Chief Concerns," 2003. www.publicagenda.org.

- The use of LSD and other hallucinogens leads to an increased chance of **miscarriage** in pregnant women. Some research also links LSD use during pregnancy to birth defects.

- Hallucinogens are not **illegal** only in the United States. They are illegal throughout most of western Europe and Australia.

Key People and Advocacy Groups

Richard Alpert: Together with Timothy Leary, Richard Alpert conducted experiments with hallucinogens, assisting with the formation of the Center for Research in Personality at Harvard. He was dismissed with Leary in 1963; however, he persisted in personal research and advocacy for spiritual growth, changed his name to Baba Ram Dass, and is now a guru.

Drug Free America Foundation: Drug Free America Foundation, Inc., is a drug prevention and policy organization committed to developing, promoting, and sustaining global strategies, policies, and laws that will reduce illegal drug use, drug addiction, and drug-related injury and death. The foundation is against the legalization of drugs because it believes legalization will lead to the greater availability of dangerous drugs in our communities and will undermine law enforcement and health care.

Drug Policy Alliance: The Drug Policy Alliance works to advance policies and attitudes that best reduce the harms of both drug misuse and drug prohibition and to promote the sovereignty of individuals over their minds and bodies.

Albert Hofmann: Albert Hofmann is a Swiss scientist sometimes referred to as the "father of LSD" because he accidentally discovered the drug while researching ergot. He recorded his experiments and experiences with LSD and wrote about them in his famous book *LSD: My Problem Child.* He has worked in recent years advocating scientific research on hallucinogens.

Timothy Leary: Inspired by a *Life* magazine article by Gordon Wasson, Leary began experimenting with psilocybin, eventually moving to LSD. He formed the Federation for Internal Freedom advocating the use of hallucinogens for personal growth. A Harvard psychology professor, he was dismissed in 1963 but continued to be important politically and culturally in the promotion of hallucinogens.

Terence McKenna: McKenna had wide-ranging interests, with degrees from the University of California at Berkeley in ecology, resource conservation, and even shamanism. He argued that hallucinogenic plants were the source of the Tree of Knowledge in the Garden of Eden presented in the biblical Book of Genesis. He and his wife began a nonprofit business to grow plants from around the world that have medicinal and spiritual significance.

Multidisciplinary Association for Psychedelic Studies (MAPS): The Multidisciplinary Association for Psychedelic Studies (MAPS) is a membership-based nonprofit research and educational organization. It helps scientists design, obtain approval for, fund, conduct, and report on research into the healing and spiritual potentials of psychedelics and marijuana.

Max Rinkel: Max Rinkel brought LSD to the United States from Switzerland's Sandoz Pharmaceuticals. Sandoz Pharmaceuticals sold LSD legally until 1966, when it was outlawed. All stock then went to the National Institute for Mental Health, a federal research center.

Alexander Shulgin: A senior research chemist for Dow Chemical Company, Alexander Shulgin has worked in biochemistry, psychiatry, and pharmacology. He has been involved in synthesis and research into the therapeutic effects of hallucinogens, especially MDMA, since 1967.

Reuben Snake: Reuben Snake was a member of the Winabago tribe and an important advocate for the Native American Church of North America. He assisted in the legalization of peyote for religious use by church members.

Richard Strassman: Richard Strassman began his research with hallucinogens while an associate professor of psychiatry at the medical school of the University of New Mexico. His work has been published in peer-reviewed journals as well as popular magazines.

Chronology

3700 B.C.
Native Americans in the Rio Grande area collect peyote buttons.

1000–500 B.C.
Central American cultures build temples to the gods who protect their mushrooms.

1799
The first medically documented mushroom experience takes place in London to a man identified in medical journals as "JS."

1912
MDMA is patented by Merck Pharmaceuticals.

1938
Albert Hofmann, a Swiss chemist working for Sandoz Pharmaceuticals synthesizes LSD-25 for the first time.

1943
Albert Hofmann accidentally ingests a small amount of LSD and records this first "trip" in his journal.

1954
The Doors of Perception by Aldous Huxley is published describing his experiences using mescaline.

B.C.   A.D.

3700   1500   1500   1800   1900   1910   1920   1930   1940   1950

1521
Use of hallucinogenic mushrooms and peyote is driven underground as the Europeans in Mexico banish the use of any nonalcoholic intoxicants.

1918
The Native American Church is formed.

1950
The first article about LSD appears in the *American Psychiatric Journal.*

1919
Mescaline is first synthesized.

1951 The CIA becomes aware of and begins experimenting with LSD.

1897
Mescaline is first isolated by German chemist Arthur Heffter.

1958 Psilocybin is first isolated from mushrooms by Albert Hofmann.

1960
Harvard University's Timothy Leary establishes the Psychedelic Research Project.

1970
The Controlled Substances Act places most hallucinogens such as mescaline and peyote on the Schedule I list; cocaine is listed as a Schedule II substance.

1988
MDMA is permanently placed on the Schedule I list of drugs by the DEA.

1963
LSD first appears on the streets.

1977
FDA-approved research on the benefits of psilocybin as a psychotherapeutic medicine ends and will not be resumed until the 1990s.

1990s
Research with hallucinogenic drugs like psilocybin experiences a resurgence in the scientific community.

1966
LSD becomes illegal in California.

| 1960 | 1965 | 1970 | 1975 | 1980 | 1985 | 1990 | 1995 | 2000 |

1961
Timothy Leary and Richard Alpert use pure psilocybin in experiments on Harvard students.

1985
MDMA is temporarily listed as a Schedule I substance by the DEA.

late 1990s
SAMHSA reports a marked increase in the number of deaths associated with MDMA.

1968
Possession of psilocybin becomes illegal in the United States.

1987
The first report of a human death from MDMA use is published.

1965
Alexander Shulgin synthesizes MDMA but does not try it.

1979
Albert Hofmann publishes the first edition of *LSD: My Problem Child.*

1967
LSD and peyote are banned in the United States.

Related Organizations

Common Sense for Drug Policy (CSDP)

1377-C Spencer Ave.

Lancaster, PA 17603

phone: (717) 299-0600 • fax: (717) 393-4953

Web site: www.csdp.org

Common Sense for Drug Policy is a nonprofit organization dedicated to reforming drug policy and expanding harm reduction. This organization disseminates factual information and comments on existing laws, policies, and practices. CSDP provides advice and assistance to individuals and organizations and facilitates coalition building. CSDP's Web site also provides links to numerous current news stories related to a variety of drugs.

Drug Abuse Resistance Education (DARE)

PO Box 512090

Los Angeles, CA 90051

phone: (800) 223-DARE or (800) 215-0575

Web site: www.dare.com

DARE's primary mission is to provide children with the information and skills they need to live drug- and violence-free lives. It also works to establish positive relationships between students and law enforcement, teachers, parents, and other community leaders. It was founded it 1983 and develops curricula to be used in K-12 classrooms.

Drug Enforcement Administration (DEA)

2401 Jefferson Davis Hwy., Suite 300

Alexandria, VA 22301

phone: (800) 882-9539 • Web site: www.dea.gov

The Drug Enforcement Administration works to enforce the controlled substances laws and regulations in the United States. The DEA coordinates with federal, state, and local law-enforcement agencies on mutual drug-enforcement efforts. It also recommends and supports programs aimed at reducing the availability and use of illicit drugs.

Drug Free America Foundation (DFAF)

2600 Ninth St., N, Suite 200

St. Petersburg, FL 33704

phone: (727) 828-0212 • Web site: www.dfaf.org

Drug Free America Foundation, Inc., is a drug prevention and policy organization committed to developing, promoting, and sustaining global strategies, policies, and laws that will reduce illegal drug use, drug addiction, and drug-related injury and death. The DFAF is against the legalization of drugs because it believes legalization will lead to the greater availability of dangerous drugs in our communities and will undermine law enforcement and health care.

Drug Policy Alliance

925 15th St. NW., 2nd Fl.

Washington, DC 20005

phone: (202) 216-0035 • e-mail: dc@drugpolicy.org

Web site: www.drugpolicy.org

The Drug Policy Alliance works to advance policies and attitudes that best reduce the harms of both drug misuse and drug prohibition, and to promote the sovereignty of individuals over their minds and bodies. The Drug Policy Alliance's library is one of the largest collections on drugs and drug policy in the world.

Drug Reform Coordination Network

1623 Connecticut Ave. NW, 3rd Fl.

Washington, DC 20009

phone: (202) 293-8340 • fax: (202) 293-8344

e-mail: drcnet@drcnet.org • Web site: http://stopthedrugwar.org

Stop the Drug War (Drug Reform Coordination Network) is an international organization working for an end to drug prohibition worldwide and for interim policy reform in U.S. drug laws and the criminal justice system. Its members consist of educators, lawyers, health-care professionals, and others who believe current drug policies should be reformed. It calls for an end to the prohibition of drugs and believes drugs that are now illegal should be regulated and controlled.

Erowid

PO Box 1116

Grass Valley, CA 95945

e-mail: sage@erowid.org • Web site: www.erowid.org

Erowid is a member-supported organization that provides access to reliable, nonjudgmental information about psychoactive plants and chemicals and related issues. It works with academic, medical, and experiential experts to develop and publish new resources and to improve and increase access to already existing resources. It also strives to ensure that these resources are maintained and preserved as a historical record for the future.

Multidisciplinary Association for Psychedelic Studies (MAPS)

10424 Love Creek Rd.

Ben Lomond, CA 95005

phone: (831) 336-4325

Web site: www.maps.org

The Multidisciplinary Association for Psychedelic Studies (MAPS) is a membership-based nonprofit research and educational organization. It helps scientists design, obtain approval for, fund, conduct, and report on research into the healing and spiritual potentials of psychedelics and marijuana.

National Drug Intelligence Center (NDIC)

Office of Policy and Interagency Affairs

United States Department of Justice

Robert F. Kennedy Bldg., Rm. 1335

950 Pennsylvania Ave. NW

Washington, DC 20530

phone: (202) 532-4040

Web site: www.usdoj.gov

Established in 1993, the National Drug Intelligence Center is a component of the U.S. Department of Justice and a member of the intelligence community. The General Counterdrug Intelligence Plan, signed by the president in February 2000, designated NDIC as the nation's principal center for strategic domestic counterdrug intelligence. Its mission is to support national policy makers and law enforcement decision makers with strategic domestic drug intelligence, to support intelligence community counterdrug efforts, and to produce national, regional, and state drug threat assessments.

National Institute on Drug Abuse (NIDA)

6001 Executive Blvd., Rm. 5213

Bethesda, MD 20892-9561

phone: (301) 443-1124

e-mail: information@nida.nih.gov • Web site: www.nida.nih.gov

The National Institute on Drug Abuse's mission is to lead the nation in bringing the power of science to bear on drug abuse and addiction. NIDA was established in 1974, and in October 1992 it became part of the National Institutes of Health, Department of Health and Human Services. The institute is organized into divisions and offices, each of which plays an important role in programs of drug abuse research.

Office of National Drug Control Policy

Drug Policy Information Clearinghouse

PO Box 6000

Rockville, MD 20849-6000

phone: (800) 666-3332 • fax: (301) 519-5212

Web site: www.whitehousedrugpolicy.gov

The White House Office of National Drug Control Policy, a component of the Executive Office of the President, was established by the Anti-Drug Abuse Act of 1988. The principal purpose of ONDCP is to establish policies, priorities, and objectives for the nation's drug control program. The goals of the program are to reduce illicit drug use, manufacturing, and trafficking, drug-related crime and violence, and drug-related health consequences. To achieve these goals, the director of ONDCP is charged with producing the National Drug Control Strategy.

For Further Research

Books

David M. Grilly, *Drugs and Human Behavior.* 4th ed. Boston: Allyn and Bacon, 2002.

Charles S. Grob, ed., *Hallucinogens: A Reader.* New York: Penguin, 2003.

Robert M. Julien, *A Primer of Drug Action.* 10th ed. New York: Worth, 2005.

Charles J. Ksir, Oakley S. Ray, and Carl L. Hart, *Drugs, Society, and Human Behavior.* New York: McGraw Hill, 2005.

Robert E. Masters and Jean Houston, *Varieties of Psychedelic Experience: The Classic Guide to the Effects of LSD on the Human Psyche.* Rochester, VT: Inner Traditions International, 2000.

Terence McKenna. *Food of the Gods: The Search for the Original Tree of Knowledge.* New York: Bantam, 1993.

Joel Miller, *Bad Trip: How the War Against Drugs Is Destroying America.* Nashville, TN: Thomas Nelson, 2004.

Robert Montgomery, *Animals and Psychedelics: The Natural World and the Instinct to Alter Consciousness.* Rochester, VT: Inner Traditions International, 2002.

Cheryl Pellerin, *Trips: How Hallucinogens Work in Your Brain.* New York: Seven Stories, 1998.

Andrew Weil and Winifred Rosen, *From Chocolate to Morphine: Everything You Need to Know About Mind-Altering Drugs.* New York: Houghton Mifflin, 2004.

Periodicals

Henry David Abraham, Andrew M. Aldridge, and Prashant Gogia, "The Psychopharmacology of Hallucinogens," *Neuropsychopharmacology,* 1996.

Bruce Bower, "Chemical Enlightenment: Line Up for the Scientific, Psychedelic Mystical Tour," *Science News,* September 2006.

Susan Brown, "Researchers Explore New Visions for Hallucinogens," *Chronicle of Higher Education*, December 2006.

Billy Cate, "Heads Ups: Real News About Drugs and Your Body," *Scholastic Choices,* October 2003.

Peter T. Furst, "Visionary Plants and Ecstatic Shamanism," *Expedition*, Spring 2004.

N. Goodman, "The Serotonergic System and Mysticism: Could LSD and the Nondrug-Induced Experience Share Common Neural Mechanisms?" *Journal of Psyhcoactive Drugs*, 2002.

Harvard Mental Health Letter, "Reviving the Study of Hallucinogens," October 2006.

John P. Hoffman and Robert A. Johnson, "A National Portrait of Family Structure and Adolescent Drug Use," *Journal of Marriage and the Family*, August 1998.

Jeffrey Kluger and Jeffrey Ressner, "Balding, Wrinkled, and Stoned," *Time*, January 2006.

Steven Kotler, "Drugs in Rehab," *Psychology Today*, March/April 2005.

Kathiann M. Kowalski, "What Hallucinogens Can Do to Your Brain," *Current Health,* April/May 2000.

Paula Kurtzweil, "Medical Possibilities for Psychedelic Drugs," *Federal Drug Administration Consumer*, September 2005.

Jill A. McCaughan et al., "From 'Candy-Kids' to 'Chemi-Kids': A Typology of Young Adults Who Attend Raves in the Midwestern United States," *Substance Use and Abuse*, March 2005.

Michael Montagne, "From Problem Child to Wonder Child: LSD Turns 50," *Newsletter of the Multidisciplinary Association for Psychedelic Studies*, Spring 1993.

Alonso G. Montoya et al., "Long-Term Neuropsychiatric Consequences of 'Ecstasy' (MDMA): A Review," *Harvard Review of Psychiatry*, July/August 2002.

Michael John Morgan, "Ecstasy (MDMA): A Review of Its Possible Persistent Psychological Effects," *Psychopharmacology*, 2000.

Hazel Muir, "Party Animals," *New Scientist*, December 2003.

Kurt B. Nolte and Ross E. Zumwalt, "Fatal Peyote Ingestion Associated with Mallory-Weiss Lacerations," *Western Journal of Medicine*, June 1999.

———*New Scientist*, "Psychedelic Healing," April 2006.

Alexander T. Shulgin, "Abused Substances," *Technology Review*, August 2005.

Eugene Taylor, "Psychedelics," *Psychology Today*, July/August 1996.

Internet Sources

John Horgan, "Tripping De-Light Fantastic: Are Psychedelic Drugs Good for You?" *Slate*, 2003. www.slate.com/id/2082647.

Howard Markel, "Ecstasy," *Medscape Pediatrics*, eMedicine, January 2004. www.emedicine.com/med/topic3407.htm.

E.J. Mishan, "Why LSD Should Be Legalized," *Schaffer Library of Drug Policy*, 1980. www.druglibrary.org/Schaffer/lsd/mishan.htm.

Office of National Drug Control Policy, "The President's National Drug Policy," 2006. www.whitehousedrugpolicy.gov/publications/policy/ndcs06/stopping_use.html.

The Vaults of Erowid, "LSD Analysis: Do We Know What's in Street Acid? 2003. www.erowid.org/chemicals/lsd/lsd-article1.shtml.

Source Notes

Overview

1. David M. Grilly, *Drugs and Human Behavior*, 4th ed. Boston: Allyn and Bacon, 2002, p. 264.
2. Sarah Pekkan, "Experts Tell FDA Some Hallucinogens May Aid Alcoholics, Terminally Ill and Psychiatric Patients," *Newsletter of the Multidisciplinary Association for Psychedelic Studies*, 1992. www.maps.org.
3. The Vaults of Erowid, "Mad Anxiety: Ecstasy & Alcohol," July 12, 2005. www.erowid.org.
4. U.S. Department of Justice, "Rise in Hallucinogen Use," *National Institute of Justice: Research in Brief*, October 1997. www.serendipity.li.
5. University of Michigan, "Trends in Lifetime Prevalence of Use of Various Drugs of Eighth, Tenth, and Twelfth Graders," Monitoring the Future, 2006. www.monitoringthefuture.org.
6. University of Michigan, "Trends in Lifetime Prevalence of Use of Various Drugs of Eighth, Tenth, and Twelfth Graders."

What Are Hallucinogens?

7. Richard Evans Schultes, "The Plant Kingdom and Hallucinogens (Part I)," August 30, 2001. http://leda.lycaeum.org.
8. William A. McKim, *Drugs and Behavior: An Introduction to Behavioral Pharmacology*, 5th ed. Upper Saddle River, NJ: Prentice Hall, 2003, p. 307.
9. Bruce Bower, "Chemical Enlightenment: Line Up for the Scientific, Psychedelic Mystical Tour," *Science News,* September 30, 2006, pp. 216–17.

How Harmful Are Hallucinogens?

10. Rick Strassman, "Hallucinogens," in *Mind-Altering Drugs: The Science of Subjective Experience,* ed. by Mitch Earleywine. New York: Oxford University Press, 2005, pp. 49–85.
11. "Psychedelic Healing," Susan Blackmore interview of Torsten Passie, *New Scientist*, April 15, 2006, pp. 50–51.
12. Ken Liska, *Drugs and the Human Body: With Implications for Society*, 7th ed. Upper Saddle River, NJ: Pearson/Prentice Hall, p. 289.
13. Strassman, "Hallucinogens," p. 57.
14. Quoted in the *Independent*, "Dr. Albert Hofmann: The Father of LSD," January 10, 2006. http://news.independent.co.uk.
15. Paul May, "Lysergic Acid Diethylamide—LSD," December 1998. www.chm.bris.ac.uk.

How Serious a Problem Are Hallucinogens for Society?

16. J. Thomas Ungerleider et al., "The 'Bad Trip'—the Etiology of the Adverse LSD Reaction," *American Journal of Psychiatry,* May 11, 1968, pp. 1,483–90.
17. Dana Hunt, "Rise of Hallucinogen Use," National Institute of Justice: *Research in Brief*, October 1997. www.ncjrs.gov.
18. Hunt, "Rise of Hallucinogen Use." www.ncjrs.gov.
19. Andrew Weil and Winifred Rosen, *From Chocolate to Morphine: Everything You Need to Know About Mind-Altering Drugs.* Boston: Houghton Mifflin, 1983, p. 107.

How Can Illegal Hallucinogens Be Controlled?

20. Richard B. Karel, "A Model Legalization Proposal," *Schaeffer Library of Drug Policy*, 1991. www.druglibrary.org.
21. Office of National Drug Control Policy, "The President's National Drug

Control Strategy," February 2006. www.whitehousedrugpolicy.gov.

22. Office of National Drug Control Policy, "The President's National Drug Control Strategy."

23. U.S. Department of Health and Human Services, Substance Abuse and Mental Health Services Administration, Center for Substance Abuse Prevention, "Keeping Youth Drug Free," 2004.

List of Illustrations

What Are Hallucinogens?

How Harmful Are Hallucinogens?

How Serious a Problem Are Hallucinogens for Society?

How Can Illegal Hallucinogens Be Controlled?

Index

About the Author

Crystal McCage holds a PhD in rhetoric from Texas Woman's University. She lives in Bend, Oregon, with her husband, Wesley, and their son Joseph. Crystal teaches writing and literature at a small college and enjoys spending time with her son.

DATE DUE